I'm Suffering...
Please Help Me

I'm Suffering...
Please Help Me

Learning to Care for the Alone and Hurting

CRYSTAL BARBIER

www.amsosad.com

The author wants to acknowledge all the help in the reading and editing of this book. Thank you, Cindy Cowherd, for your valued help on this project.

I'm Suffering...
Please Help Me
Learning to Care for the Alone and Hurting
Copyright © 2014 by Crystal Barbier
All rights reserved.
www.amsosad.com
Peruse My Shop, LLC,
2131 Woodruff Rd, Ste 2100, #155,
Greenville, SC 29607

Cover design by Cindy Cowherd.

Scripture quotations are from:
"Scripture taken from the NEW AMERICAN STANDARD BIBLE, ©1960, 1962, 1963, 1968, 1971, 1972, 1973, 1975, 1977, by The Lockman Foundation. Used by permission. Scripture quotations marked (NIV) are:
"Scripture quotations taken from The Holy Bible, New International Version® NIV®, Copyright © 1973, 1978, 1984, 2011 by Biblica, Inc.™.
Used by permission. All rights reserved worldwide."
"Scripture quotations marked NLT are taken from the *Holy Bible*, New Living Translation, copyright © 1996, 2004. Used by permission of Tyndale Publishers, Inc., Wheaton, Illinois 60189. All rights reserved."

Printed in the United States of America

ISBN 978-1-941275-00-9

Dedication

This book is lovingly dedicated to my Lord

who has given me mercy and strength,

to my children who have brought me joy,

to my dear friends

who have demonstrated to me the love of Christ,

and to my brother who has helped me

each step along the way.

A good character is the best tombstone.

Those who loved you and were helped by you

will remember you

when forget-me-nots have withered.

Carve your name on hearts, not on marble.

–Charles H. Spurgeon

Table of Contents

"I have known Crystal Barbier for more than 20 years. It struck me while I was reading her book that she and her son have been without their husband/father and daughter/sister for half of those years now. Readers of Crystal's book will be allowed to share in the unimaginable pain and suffering she felt at losing half her family in a tragic car accident. The honesty with which she describes her reactions and her long walk out of overwhelming grief and pain is both refreshing and agonizing. Refreshing, because that painfully honest recounting of loss and recovery is often glossed over when Christians talk about grief. Agonizing, because she spares no detail in sharing her difficult story. Crystal offers practical help in how to love those lost in their pain. She candidly explains what to say, what not to say, what is helpful, and what is not. Crystal's life is proof that God's grace is sufficient in suffering."

–Debbe Mays, Women and Families Counselor

Introduction

Most people view their lives with hope embedded in the future. A parent has a child and may raise their child with the desire for future relationship and possibly even future joyful relationship with their grandchildren. A child may aspire to have health, independence, and long life. A brother or sister may have the expectation of good family relationship. A friend may have the prospect of a life-long buddy. Most people have the hope of good health, career possibilities, long life, and enjoyment.

Sometimes that hopeful expectation is quite drastically changed by the reality of suffering.

Each one of us has a story and that story is just one of thousands. The daily news tell us of children who are born with no hope of a good story, children who are stolen from their parents, children who live in bondage, and children who die at a young age. We hear of parents who have lost their children, mothers and fathers who have a tragic accident losing their health or life, illness that destroys the health of a family member, random shootings that take away a family member, relationships that become destructive, and war injuries that change health or abilities. Natural disasters such as hurricanes, floods, fire, and earthquakes impact the lives of many. Along with each area of suffering comes the agony of pain, exhaustion due to lack of sleep, volatility of emotions, disruption of normality, loss of health, or loss of purpose.

The one who is suffering cries out for comfort. One may cry out in silence and another may cry out loud.

True comfort can be the very thing that helps the suffering determine a sense of a "new normal". What does comfort that is true, kind, and full of gentleness look like? And what is hope for the sufferer which encourages that one to go on living?

–Crystal Barbier

CHAPTER 1

Unexpected Tragedy

Many of us are familiar with the phrase, "the straw that broke the camel's back". This phrase is a description of a series of small events (burdens) that take place with the culmination of an event that is very small and yet it breaks the back of a camel, this burden bearing beast. Some people have a succession of little areas of suffering that culminates in something small which inevitably crushes them under the burden of suffering. Others have a succession of suffering that is comparable to a crescendo: the first thing that happens is small, the next is a little bigger, the following is even larger until finally there is a smashing event that causes horrific agony and excruciating pain.

Often, there will be a precedent of suffering that people have already experienced, prior to the suffering that is more visible to others in the person's life. People do not always share all the dark things that have happened to them. There may be feelings of shame and embarrassment. It could be, there has been the pressing down of verbal abuse. Or, maybe there has been control with insisted submission from the abuser. Perhaps, there are consequences from following the wrong desires of one's own heart.

Whatever the case, suffering can affect every part of the human spirit through physical and/or emotional pain. Sometimes this pain is minimal. At times, it is bearable. It is possible this pain is more than can be endured and the one suffering is broken.

My life has been comparable to both "the straw that broke the camel's back" and the "crescendo". Beginning this story with my adult life does not alleviate any prior "straws" but accepts them as the foundation to where I begin my story.

When I was 17, I left home to attend college. College life was extremely busy with classes, study, work, room-mates, and special events. Like many college kids, this was where I met my future spouse. I met Matt at the beginning of my senior year. Matt was a semester ahead of me and had graduated a year earlier. After graduation, he went back home to work and save money for our marriage. I finished my last semester, worked for a semester, and planned our wedding which was to take place on my graduation day.

The day of our marriage, May 16, 1981, was both an exhilarating and exhausting day. I graduated from college in the morning, had a surprise visit from my only living grandmother (who flew across the country for this special day), put together my flowers for the wedding in the afternoon (with the help of some friends), while visiting with my grandmother, and was married at 7 p.m. in the evening.

We started our marriage with a "crash". About three hours after our wedding, we sat on an interstate outside Pensacola, Florida, in a wrecked car, waiting to be transported to the emergency room at a nearby hospital. We had cars lined up behind the wreck, a helicopter flying overhead (waiting to take us if necessary), and the kindness of a truck driver who had called in the wreck. We were on our way to Mobile, Alabama, from our wedding, when we had a head-on collision with a young, drunk fellow who happened to be parked on the interstate. Our new Volkswagon Rabbit was designed in such a way that the front wheels would collapse and keep the engine from landing on the front seat in a head-on collision. Well, it worked!

Matt and I were both in pain. Spending the majority of the night in the emergency room on our honeymoon night was definitely not the plan. Both of us had injuries that would take some time to heal. Matt's thumb was broken and placed in a cast. My collar bone and some ribs were broken. But, it did not seem so bad. We were young and optimistic regarding the future.

To this day, I do not know what the original honeymoon plans had been. Matt's parents had loaned us an old Volkswagon Bug to drive until we could purchase a replacement car. Some friends, who lived in the Alabama countryside, offered us their home while they were out of town. We decided to refinish their kitchen cabinets for them while they were gone. It was fun bringing joy to these friends.

After finalizing insurance details and moving to where we had decided to live, married life began.

Two weeks after our marriage, I was joyfully expecting our first child. Ten months after our marriage we had a little boy. Karl was sick most of the time, the first two years of his life. As a result, he ended up having surgery on his ears which finally enabled him to begin growing.

Four years after our son was born, we had a little girl, Anna. She was like me all over again, including her strong will. We named our daughter, Anna Ruth, which means "gracious friend". Anna was like three kids rolled into one. She was everywhere from the time she could move. She even walked at nine months old. We were able to train Karl to obey with discipline and instruction, but with Anna, though we worked at it, we felt like we were getting nowhere. Anna was cheerfully disobedient.

The months and years rolled by and soon it was the fall of 1987. The "crescendo" had been building and life was very difficult. Karl was in kindergarten and Anna was 18 months old. On Labor Day, we took the kids to a fair. It was such an enjoyable day. We headed home late in the afternoon. I was so tired. I remember thinking how nice it would be to go to sleep.

We were almost home when we had a terrible car wreck. A lady, driving an old, red Camaro, plowed into the passenger side of our new Volkswagon Golf, driving the whole side of the car (and me) a third of the way into the car. Matt, who had been driving, was knocked out. Karl, who had been sitting behind Matt, had his foot stuck under the seat. Anna, who was sitting behind me, bumped her head when her car seat flipped. I don't remember the wreck. I don't remember screaming and screaming (as I was told) when my body was smashed.

"When I awoke after the accident, Crystal was screaming and thrashing around in obviously intense pain.

A man was in the back seat trying to calm her down and put an oxygen mask on her. I tried to keep her calmed down.

A man reached through the driver's window to put an IV into Crystal's arm. He grasped her arm. She wrenched free and tightly gripped the steering wheel. I was told to loosen her hand and hold her arm so the IV could be installed.

In the process, Crystal grabbed my left arm just below the elbow in a grip so strong that I had bruise marks (of finger imprints) for several days.

My arm was sore from where she grabbed it.

Crystal was telling people not to touch her."

–Matt Barbier, September 7, 1987

I don't remember that it took EMS 26 minutes to extract me from the wrecked car. I don't remember being told I wouldn't live to make it to the hospital, not to mention living the 45 minutes it took to drive to the hospital.

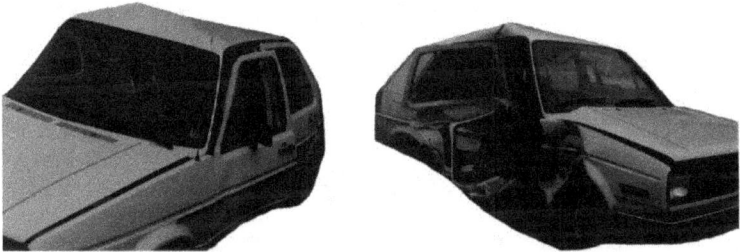

I had internal head injuries, deep cuts in the head, blood coming out my ear, a broken inner ear bone, and collapsed lung. All of my ribs on the left side were broken next to the spine. My spleen was ruptured. I had a damaged kidney. There were multiple breaks in the pelvic bone and the nerves running through the pelvic bone to my left leg were severed. My lacerated liver was like mush and there was severe bruising over my entire body. I spent several hours in surgery where my spleen was removed and foam was sprayed around my liver to act as a cast, so it could heal. It took over 2 hours of working with the liver for this foam to set. I was placed in ICU on life support under a drug-induced coma for the first week of my long hospital stay.

I have a flash memory of Matt sitting by my bed, a pastor visiting me, and of being so thirsty. This concludes my entire memory for the first week in ICU.

The wreck happened on a Monday. On the following Monday, I was brought out of a drug-induced coma and put into a regular hospital room. My Mom came, stayed in the hospital, and helped care for me, as the nurses were short-staffed. Most of the time, I could do nothing to help myself, including pulling myself up in my bed. My Mom bathed me and cared for me like I was a baby.

Every fiber of my body was in excruciating pain. My legs were black. It hurt to breath. I could not walk. I could not pull myself up in bed if I slid down in the sheets. My hair still had dried blood in it from the wreck. No one was telling me that they still did not expect me to live. A group of doctors were treating me. Often, they could not agree on the treatment. One doctor would tell me that I needed to be up walking or my lungs would deteriorate even more. As if, I could jump out of bed and walk? Another would tell me that I needed to blow harder when they exercised my lungs, which was excruciating with all of my broken ribs. One lung kept filling with fluid, so, they stuck a needle in my back to pull out over a pint of liquid. The inability of being able to breathe was frightening. A nurse friend was afraid they would puncture my lungs with the broken ribs as they pounded on my lungs to exercise them. I remember saying, like a broken record, "It hurts, It hurts, It hurts." Daily blood tests, cat scans, x-rays, and so on, were difficult to endure with that level of pain throughout my body. My veins began to break down and it was difficult to insert a new IV. Daily shots of blood thinner into my abdomen resulted in well over 100 shots by the time I was released from the hospital (after 39 days). My abdomen was covered with needle tracks. It became more and more difficult to find a bare spot of skin that didn't bleed when a shot was administered.

As the days passed and fever increased, it was determined that my liver was abscessed. A tube was inserted into my liver, connected to a bag hanging on the outside of my body, in order to drain the abscess, so the liver would heal.

"Around 6 p.m. Crystal tried to call me at work. I called back and knew something was seriously wrong. She was crying as she told me the pain she was in since they had reinstalled tubes around her liver. (I've never seen Crystal like this and knew the pain was unbelievable.)

I called my weekend job and said I couldn't work because Crystal needed me. At around 9 p.m. I arrived at the hospital in time to see an intern installing a tube to drain air off the outside of the lung. I walked outside the room and heard her cry out in pain. The look of pain on her face is etched in my mind. I've never seen her in such agony. The chest tube hurt much more than the other tubes (which she'd been in agony over before). I spent the weekend with her—a terrible, extremely painful weekend."

–Matt Barbier, October 2, 1987

People used to talk about the pain that would be endured during childbirth, before my son was born. That was a walk in the park compared to the indescribable head-to-toe pain I experienced.

During this time, friends whom we did not know well—Philip and Judy—took my husband and children into their home, for over a month. They had four boys of their own; the two youngest were the same age as our two children. Circumstances such as these will bring "dear friends" out of "friends whom we did not know well".

Along with the physical pain was the sadness of not being able to be with my children. I missed them terribly. Our son would come to visit, ride my bed up and down, and beg me to come home. Our daughter had attached herself to our friend, Judy, who was caring for her, and would have nothing to do with me. Before the accident, Anna had been a Mommy's girl. Matt was a regular visitor to the hospital, even though he was still working 70 hours a week and studying for his master's degree at Clemson University.

In an odd sort of way, I would detach myself from the suffering, almost like an observer watching myself suffer. I did become very depressed and it was difficult even to smile. I believe it was a natural reaction due to the illness and injury in my body, together with the amount of drugs that were used to counter the infection and the pain.

Someone brought me a cassette player and a "Twila Paris" cassette. On it was a song "We Will Glorify" which I rewound and listened to over and over and over.

There was no question in my mind about trusting God. Who else would I trust? I had already learned that God was sovereign, and according to His providence, I was in that hospital bed. During that time, God was purifying my life of areas that were not wholeheartedly for Him. For that, I will always be thankful.

In the midst of all of the suffering, there was therapy and learning how to walk again with a broken hip. My daily therapy became a huge area of encouragement. A young Christian lady was my therapist. We talked constantly about the Lord. She asked me regularly what I was learning, which was a difficult question to answer. It took everything in me and a strength outside of myself just to deal with the excruciating pain. The first week in the hospital I lost 20 pounds. Someone brought a pair of slacks from home for me to wear during the therapy sessions. My therapist gathered the waistband in her hands and held my pants up while she steadied me and helped me take steps. She was so gentle and patient. I really looked forward to these daily sessions.

Almost six weeks after the accident, the day finally came when I was released from the hospital. One of my doctors came into my hospital room to give me instructtions. He told me that they had not expected me to live. He said that if this wreck had happened fifteen years earlier, they would not have been able to help me with my liver injuries. During those fifteen years, there had been so many advances in treating liver injuries. The doctor told me that there was a 50 percent mortality rate just with my liver injury. The instructions continued with caution for my immune system due to the removal of my spleen. He told me to stay away from anyone with bronchitis or pneumonia, since these two things could be deadly for me. He also cautioned me to have the regular pneumococcal vaccination every 5-7 years as a preventative measure against contraction of pneumonia.

In order to be discharged from the hospital, I was given an order for several pieces of medical equipment. These items were 1 tub bench, 1 elevating commode seat, 1 hand-held shower attachment, and 1 hospital bed. The order read as follows:

She needs these items because she:
1. Has pulmonary injuries and has to sleep with her head elevated.
2. She can use only limited weight bearing to her lower extremities due to a pelvic fracture.
3. She has difficulty getting in and out of bed. A wedge used to elevate her head above bed has been ineffective.

Prior to the accident my activity could have been compared to the "energizer bunny". My extended family would tell you that my normal had been the ability to accomplish the work of several people. After the accident, it took all my energy to just take a step, let alone do any work. Although six weeks had passed, the pain was still excruciating. My legs were still covered with a black hue. Exhaustion and pain were in every move I made. My parents stayed with us for a couple of weeks after I came home. Then, I was on my own with two little children and a husband who was working 70 hours a week along with traveling to school a couple of hours from our home.

For months after I came home, the kids and I struggled with the aftermath of the accident. I had terrible abdominal pain. I would often curl up in a fetal position on the floor, unable to move. There were times it felt like a knife was stuck in my side between two of my ribs, which still reoccurs due to a rib that healed in its broken position. My strength was limited in caring for my children. Karl struggled with insecurity. Anna had terrible temper tantrums and was terrified if she didn't see me.

My physical therapy at home really began with the purchase and moving of an old 1939 mill house onto our land. This began "years" of the hard work of restoration and adding new construction. My husband tore the old construction apart and replaced both the wiring and plumbing. I rebuilt the old parts of the house and built the new construction. Of course, our children were always a huge help.

The old mill house was moved in two parts, set back together, and placed on wood pilings while a foundation was built. When the foundation was completed, the house was set down on the foundation and the pilings were removed. This still left the two parts of the house to be tied together. Each of the two parts was supported in the openings by 4 x 6 beams. I tied the rafters and the floor joists together and proceeded to remove the 4 x 6 beams. As I was removing one of them, it fell on my once broken hip. Later, I found out that I had knocked it out of place and this began many journeys to a chiropractor.

During this time, Matt found a job at Fluor Daniel, now Fluor. Matt began traveling to many places around the world with Fluor, such as Canada, Indonesia, Puerto Rico, and many parts of the United States.

As the years went by, and our children continued to grow, there were more car wrecks, an abdominal surgery to fix the cause of the continual abdominal pain, and the inability to have more children due to my injuries.

During all of this, we homeschooled and still worked on the house. We added on a 20x40 foot length which housed our three bedrooms. Later on, we added a couple of bonus rooms and a double car garage with a second story. This was for a computer business that Matt and Karl were conducting. We lived in a partially completed home

with very little furniture and no kitchen. All of our belongings were in boxes. For twelve years, I carried water
to the kitchen to wash and rinse the dishes. Life was
difficult.

This wreck changed my health and my life. My memory and my hearing were greatly affected due to head
injuries. My hip has never been normal and can be aggra-
vating, even painful. The level of pain I endured for years,
after this wreck, was at times, exhausting. Even today, a
recovery time is needed after being around a lot of
people.

Any area of suffering never seems to come in just one
avenue. It seems that one is touched in multiple ways
which increases the "crescendo".

CHAPTER 2

I'm Reeling

"God has made my heart faint, timid and broken—
but He is unchangeable, and who can turn Him?
And what He wants to do, that He does.
For He performs that which He has planned for me..."
—See Job 23:13, 14, 16
—Peaks and Valleys, Grace Gospel Publishers

As I walked forward through the following years, there were "straws" and more "straws" and then the "crescendo" hit the high in December of 2003. I thought that I knew and understood how to deal with pain, that wearying physical pain that can affect your emotions and your rest. I learned that the pain that I knew was nothing compared to what happened in December of 2003.

May 16, 2003, marked our twenty-second wedding anniversary. Matt had just finished working on a project in Puerto Rico and was beginning another project in Houston, Texas, which prefaced the beginning of the building of a huge oil refinery on the Russian Island of Sakhalin. Because of his schedule and the disorganization of the early part of the project, he did not make it home for Thanksgiving that year.

On Thursday, December 19, 2003, Matt left Houston and headed home. Early Saturday morning, Karl, Anna, and I left home and headed for Georgia, to meet Matt on his way home. We had planned to visit dear friends near Columbus, Georgia, particularly, since the man of the house had just come home from Iraq.

We chatted by cell phone all Saturday morning. We all arrived that afternoon and met at a motel that Matt had reserved. Matt was exhausted after working all day Friday and driving all Friday night through Saturday morning to meet us. After checking in at the motel, we all went to our friend's home. Matt was so exhausted that he slept most of the day. Anna and their oldest daughter were the best of friends and spent the day busy, busy, busy.

Early Sunday morning, we drove to Anniston, Alabama, to attend a small Presbyterian church there. The service was Christ-centered. Anna took notes, as the pastor preached, on how to follow the Lord Jesus by repenting of sin, bowing the knee to the Lord Jesus, and fixing one's eyes on Christ. Matt was smiling and nodding encouragement as the pastor spoke. It was a wonderful service and time of fellowship afterwards. Who would have thought that this was to be their last worship service on earth?!

That afternoon we stopped to visit friends near Lineville, Alabama. These friends were the grandparents of Anna's friend whom we had just visited. Matt, again, lay down and slept for about three hours, as did Karl. Anna and I went to visit the great grandmother who was dying of cancer. Anna always made little things to cheer her up. This time she had made her a rag doll for Christmas. She had also taken a pine cone and woven moss in between each of the petals so that she could have a Christmas tree by her bed. And then, we came back, woke Matt and Karl, said our goodbyes, and headed for home.

Matt and Anna were riding in Matt's rental car. Anna did not want her Dad to be alone. The seats in Matt's car were hurting my back, so I rode with Karl. Anna never thought of herself, only others.

Within half of an hour Matt was in heaven and Anna shortly after, both of which were unknown to Karl and me. We lost sight of Matt's car right before we got on the interstate. From then, until we arrived home, we called and called on the cell phone, with no answer.

Karl and I arrived home around 11 P.M., cooked a pizza, and ate supper. Originally, we were supposed to stop and eat supper together as a family. Inside, I was troubled. Something was wrong. I even thought we were never going to see them again. And then, I assured myself, that Matt probably pulled off to sleep at some point.

Karl went to bed, because he had to work the next day. I stayed up and waited. Around 1:30 in the morning, the doorbell rang. Upon opening the door, I saw a police car pulled up to my front door and an officer standing in front of me. "May I come in," he said. "I have bad news." "Why do you want to come in?" I said. "Ma'am, please, may I come in, I have bad news," the officer said again. I opened the door wider and let him in. He told me there was a terrible car wreck and a Matt Barbier was dead. Did I know him? I told him that was my husband. He said that there was also an unidentified female occupant in the car and she was dead. I told him that my daughter was riding with my husband. I asked the officer if he was kidding, and then again, was he sure he was not kidding. The officer then asked me if there was anyone else in the house. I told him that my son was sleeping. I ran back to Karl's room and urgently told him to get up and we went quickly back to the living room. I asked the officer to tell Karl everything he had just told me.

At first, I was in shock. I cannot explain it, but inside of me was a feeling that I had not expected to see Matt and Anna again. It was as if I knew they were already gone. I was not surprised that the officer knocked on my door, and yet, at the same time, there was disbelief. It was so surreal. When he told me they were dead, I just started shaking and did not utter a cry.

The officer gave us information regarding the police station in Alabama where we could acquire more details. Evidently, the wreck occurred after going 8 miles on I-20, towards Atlanta, from their entrance point onto I-20.

After the officer left we called the police station in Alabama and they said that Matt had died instantly and that Anna was still alive. Karl immediately started getting our belongings together so that we could get in the car, as quickly as possible, and travel the four and a half hours back. They said that Anna was at the hospital in Birming-ham, but when we called, she wasn't there. We finally found her and identified her at Anniston Regional. The doctors were waiting to transport her to the Birmingham trauma center. They would not tell us anything about her condition, which was troubling.

I told Karl that we had to make phone calls before we went. I called Matt's parents, my parents, our friends whom we had just left in Alabama/Georgia, and a couple of people in our church. This took about an hour before we could finally get going. Already I was alternately weeping and shaking, trying to tell people what happened. Karl was so kind and so much a man. He just took charge and talked when I could not talk and had everything ready to go by the time the phone calls were made.

We had just driven a few miles from our house, when our elder called. He told us to go to our dear friend John's house where he would meet us and they both would drive us to Birmingham. At first, I just wanted to keep going, but Karl assured me that we needed to let them do this. When we arrived at John's house our pastor was there and waiting to pray with us before we left.

John and our elder took care of everything, alternately driving, answering phone calls, and taking care of details. I am so thankful for their kindness and love demonstrated that day and during the days that followed. Most of the time, during the rest of the night and the next day, all four of our cell phones were busy.

A couple of hours down the road, we were able to get a hold of one of the trauma doctors in Birmingham who was working with Anna. The only thing he would tell us was to hurry up and get there. He said that Anna had brain damage with bleeding in and around the brain, her lungs would not stay inflated, and they could not keep her blood oxygen levels up. During the time we were driving (we found out later), many people in our church stayed up the rest of the night, praying for us, and waiting to find out any news available as we traveled.

We arrived at the hospital in Birmingham early Monday morning, found where we needed to go, and asked to see Anna. We walked into her hospital room where a private nurse was standing by her bed. Anna was covered with a thick cover. They said that they had to warm her body up when she came in from Anniston Regional. I thought that was kind of funny. She had a tube coming out of her mouth and her lips were pursed Anna style. A machine was pumping her heart. She looked like she was asleep. But, when I looked at her, my spirit within knew that she was not there. She was gone. It was her body we were looking at. She wasn't there. I don't remember all the series of events. We were there until noon. We still did not know all the details of what happened.

Anna's nurse said that they were pushed down the road by a semi truck. The doctor said that the impact of the wreck was so great that it snapped Anna's brain stem. The brain was unable to tell the body what to do. By the time we saw her, her body temperature wasn't even up to normal, her blood was seeping throughout her body, they could not keep oxygen levels up in her blood, and so the news continued. Her doctors showed us her brain scans and the brain scans of a normal brain. They said that there was not a shred of hope, which was my concern. If John and our elder had not been with us, I don't know what we would have done. Their encouragement and the strength from the Lord helped us to bravely decide what we needed to do.

It was at this point that I realized they wanted Anna to be a donor. After discussing this matter with them, we made the necessary arrangements. Our elder called a dear doctor friend, to ask his advice regarding Anna's condition. Our doctor friend told me, "I think you know that she is already gone and has been for some time." This, I knew in my heart. Our doctor friend told me later, while he was talking to the nurse on the phone and getting Anna's stats, he was crying. Earlier, he had been in surgery, when his wife called to tell him that Matt was dead. He had a patient open on the table, yet took a few minutes aside privately, with tears, before finishing the surgery.

The head nurse, with whom we were making donor arrangements, spoke to us about grieving and encouraged us to hang onto whatever would make us feel better; to some people that was God, to others, other comforts. Into my head and out of my mouth popped the verse, "Absent from the body is present with the Lord" (2 Corinthians 5:8).

26

Right around noon, as we were leaving the hospital, some Furman kids (home for Christmas) that Karl knew through RUF (Reformed University Fellowship) met us. They came to encourage Karl. They also brought us a plate of ham sandwiches. At this point, we were numb, so very sad, and yet, thankful for their kindness.

We left the hospital, driving back to Anniston in search of Matt's body, the wrecked car, and any information we could attain regarding the accident. My older brother located the car, EMS, and the mortician. After seeing the car (which was absolutely a twisted mass of metal from the back end to the front seat) and speaking to the EMS people, we were able to put together some of the details of the wreck.

The traffic that night before was Christmas traffic. Cars were traveling bumper to bumper at around 85 miles per hour. Evidently Matt made contact with a semi truck as he was moving into the left lane. The semi truck picked him up and pushed him down the road at 85 miles an hour. When the driver realized he was pushing their car and backed off, the wheels on Matt's car grabbed, throwing him, at 85 miles an hour, across the median into oncoming traffic. As he flew, he spun, and was rear-ended from the passenger corner of the car by a Ford Explorer.

The EMS fellow that pulled Matt out of the car said that Matt was dead on impact and they could not resuscitate him. He only expelled air when he was moved. They saw that as normal for a severe brute force trauma victim. When they took Anna's pulse, she was breathing normally at 20 times per minute. When they took her out of the car and put a tube down her throat into her lungs for oxygen, her lungs collapsed like popping a paper bag. All of her body levels started going down and they were never able to get them back up again. Evidently her headrest had broken on one side. That, along with the force of impact (like hitting a block wall at 160 miles per hour) is what snapped her brain stem, which the EMS did not know at that time.

From everything I was told, I believe Anna went to be with the Lord shortly after. They kept her heart going with machines, but she was not there. The EMS said the wreck was so bad that traffic going both directions was backed up for over two hours.

When we found the mortician we were not allowed to see Matt's body. They were already embalming him.

After that, we met a younger brother of mine, ate supper and headed home. We arrived at John's house to find all the elders and their wives from our church waiting to hug us. It was so quiet. I was thinking that it was like a funeral procession, which of course, it was.

It wasn't long until the crying began. In just a short time, there were so many people. People were calling on the phone, bringing food to the house, asking what they could do, and wanting decisions made. Others had their own sorrow with the loss of Matt and Anna. That week was filled with people coming and going. Family and friends came in from all over the U.S. and Canada. Others called from around the world, due to all of Matt's traveling.

This awful blow sent me into a state of shock. It was like walking in a daze. I got up early in the morning to the phone ringing and it never stopped ringing. I was over-whelmed that all my brothers, sister, Matt's brothers, sister, and, of course, our parents came. I couldn't sleep. It was hard to eat. Every fiber within was hurting. My heart was in agony. It was not tangible like the car wreck where I was physically injured. Physical pain is tangible; emotional pain is intangible. I wept throughout the night, got up each morning and wept more. When others were around, it was like a mask was plastered on my face and behind the mask was sorrow. My mind would not work. I couldn't think. I couldn't focus. I heard what people said, but it didn't register. I couldn't remember what they said. Their words would not stay in my mind. It was so hard to make decisions. Again, it was like I was observing myself suffer and yet the separation wasn't as distinct. The pain was horrific.

On Christmas morning I opened my eyes to find a wrapped package by my bed. My son had spent the night preparing framed pictures of our family. I will never forget the tenderness of this special gift. Oh, how I wept.

The funeral came and went. People went back to their homes. My sister stayed for a little while and then left. And there I was, all alone. One day I had a family and the next day...

My son did not want to be there anymore. More and more, he stayed away from home. I really was physically all alone.

The flood of tears increased. I could not stop. I must have filled up hundreds of bottles with my tears. For months I did not sleep. I was exhausted. I would go to bed and listen to music to remind myself of the character of God, His mercies, and His goodness, but I could not pray. And yet, I felt this deep abiding peace alongside this horrible agony within. I was in a pit so deep I could not help myself.

Grief is like being on a precipice and standing on loose gravel near the edge. One roll of a stone and you are falling into a deep cavern below. I had fallen and was in that cavern.

This was the crescendo. The worst fears, that any spouse or parent could have, had been realized in my life. People commented on how strong I was at the funeral, but I was just in shock and reeling from the impact of such a blow. Truly, anything that people saw was only the grace of God carrying me.

Then, the tormenting thoughts began. What if? Will I forget what Anna looks like? I couldn't protect my daughter! How will my son fare when I am gone? How can I help him when I can't even help myself? This can't be true. No, this isn't true. Wait a minute...and then the reality hits you again; the agony is fresh and new as if it just happened. I was a wife and a mother. What am I supposed to do now? I was scared and helpless, sometimes frantic! What was normal? How could I ever feel "alive" again?

There were the inevitable regrets that flooded my mind, of things not done, things that should have been done, or things that were wrongly done. Thankfully, over time, the Lord has been faithful to bring sins to my mind that needed repentance and the forgiveness of the Lord.

Grief can be likened to falling in love. When one falls in love, there are heightened feelings and a rush of love often defined as passion. Initially, that love exists in this state of heightened feeling. Then, as time passes, love deepens and becomes comfortable as one settles into married life. From time to time there is still that rush of deep love or passion, but most of the time it is comfortable and settled. Grief is similar. It hits one with shock impact. It hurts so deep that it is agony. The heightened feeling of pain is excruciating and envelopes every waking moment. Then, as time passes, it settles in to stay and becomes a dull and constant ache. It is a reminder of the missing loved one(s). It is there to stay and doesn't go away. From time to time there is a memory, an occasion, a person that initiates that deep and painful agony. But, for the most part, the pain of grief has settled in to stay.

Grief brings exhaustion. It takes its toll on a person in so many ways physically. The accumulating months of sleeplessness made it even harder to sleep and exhausttion became embedded within affecting my emotions even more, as well as my desire to live.

During the nights, I listened to Michael Card and Stephen Eager over and over as they sang about the character and promises of God. The piercing truths caused me to weep even more. During the days I lived in the Psalms. It was the only part of the Scripture where my heart and mind found comfort.

In the midst of all of this there were thank you notes to write. It was so hard to do. I couldn't write very many in a day. It just made me weep more. Sometimes, even though I tried to put one foot in front of the other, I would just curl up in bed in a fetal position and weep. I felt so weak and helpless. Even in this condition, I felt a deep peace along-side this agonizing pain.

Besides the death of two members of my family at Christmas time, was the condition of my home, which was so depressing. Everything needed to be completed; everything was a mess besides the unfinished construction. My belongings were in boxes. The majority of the living room had unfinished hardwood floor stacked waste high. My bedroom was full of tools and supplies. The dining room was stacked with boxes and there were two desks sandwiched amongst the boxes with the guys' computers. The area over the garage was enclosed and sided but not framed up or finished on the inside. And still, no kitchen with running water.

As I began to work on the house, everything I did I had to redo, sometimes even redo a third time.

The emptiness and loneliness, that only loved ones can fill, was overwhelming. It hurt to be around people. It hurt to be by myself. Everything was agony. I could hardly stand to be around a family with a daughter the same age as Anna. It hurt so bad!

To this day, I have not corrected Anna's school work which came to an abrupt close on the day of her death. Anna was half way through her senior year of high school.

The loss did not stop with my family but continued on as I watched a best friend die of cancer. My church had a large split and many other friends were gone. There was much dissension and it hurt. And then, my son and I were the ones to leave our church. Others withdrew their friendship and many other friends dropped away (who were still considered dear friends). I lost another best friend. It was loss after loss after loss. The aloneness was greater than ever.

During all of this time, even up through today, there has been no one that could say that they understood what it was like to lose a husband/daughter or a dad/sister at one time. The deep cavern that I was in just seemed to get deeper. I have never been so low in all of my life.

I believe the Lord carried me through all these difficult days as my son and I began the long walk of learning how to go forward without the rest of our family.

"Even to your old age, I shall be the same, and even to your graying years I shall bear you! I have done it, and I shall carry you; and I shall bear you and I shall deliver you" (Isaiah 46:4).

Walking forward (living) with all the pain and depth of emotions due to physical and relational loss sometimes causes the questions of faith and life to arise.

CHAPTER 3

Why Do We Suffer?

"You don't have a soul. You are a Soul. You have a body."

"A man can no more diminish God's glory
by refusing to worship Him
than a lunatic can put out the sun
by scribbling the word,
'darkness' on the walls of his cell."
—C. S. Lewis
(British Scholar and Novelist. 1898-1963)

Some of the questions that sometimes arise out of suffering are: "Why?" "Why me?" "Why must I suffer?" "Why can't I have a nice life?" These questions flow out of a number of ways of thinking.

The first way of thinking is founded on the philosophy built in America based on our theory of life. Many people believe in the "American Dream" which is a successful business, the correct neighborhood, the newest style of home, a newer car in the garage, a good family, the best schools for the kids, the right friends, time to have pleasure, and a nice life. Because of this philosophy and the many successes in our country, people still come from all over the world with the desire of becoming a citizen and having that better life. This is the land of possibility. This is the land where people can thrive and grow without some of the life-threatening situations in other countries. This is a place where one can prosper.

The second way of thinking is founded on the philosophy that all people are inherently good. Because people are inherently good, bad things should not happen to good people. In other words, we deserve something better. We do not deserve to suffer.

Both of these philosophies are truly rooted in self-centered desires. The first way of thinking tells me that I cannot be happy or be joyful "unless" I have a successful job, the correct neighborhood, a fashionable house, the latest automobile, a good family, the right friends, or fun times. The second way of thinking declares its happiness or joy to be founded on the fact that a person's goodness is great enough that no suffering is deserved or acceptable.

The third and fourth ways of thinking are directed at the person who is suffering. Sometimes suffering "does" flow out of wrongdoing or sin in the form of consequences. If I steal from the grocery store, I will be prosecuted for stealing and receive a sentence for my wrongdoing. If I harm my neighbor, I will be prosecuted and receive a sentence for my wrongdoing. There may be other consequences that follow with time as my sin affects others in my life.

This final way of thinking is demonstrated in the book of Job in the Old Testament (Bible). Job is a man who lost his ten children to death, his wealth to natural disaster and thievery, his status in the community, his health, and even the confidence of his wife. Job's friends over the course of several days proceeded to try to figure out what sins Job had committed so that they could attribute all of these sufferings to his sinful actions. The conclusion of Job's friends lies in the theory that all suffering can be directly related to a person's wrong doing. The problem with this way of thinking is that God and Job knew that Job had not sinned (Job 1:1). God purposed Job's suffering to demonstrate Job's faithfulness and trust in Him. Ultimately, this demonstrated the glory of God. It was God who made Job faithful. Not only did God say that Job turned away from evil (large hint), God also declared that Job was the most righteous man on the face of the earth at that time (Job 1:8).

The question "Why Do We Suffer?" directly or indirectly poses the premise that the focus, at some point, is on "self." If we are truly inherently "good", then we cannot simultaneously do anything wrong. If we have done one thing wrong or sinned one time i.e. a lie, a lustful thought, taking something that belongs to another, saying something bad about another, etc., then we cannot claim to be inherently good. What if the following questions were asked instead: "Why not me?" "Why shouldn't I suffer?" "What causes me to think I deserve to have health, wealth, and happiness?" "What can I learn from suffering?" "What can be gained from suffering?" "How can I rejoice in suffering?" "How can I be thankful in suffering?" "How can I minister to others through my suffering?"

Instead of the question "Why Do We Suffer?" we must look at "who" suffered. The "who" is Jesus Christ—the God who created us (John 1:1-3, 9-10), the God who became man (John 1:14-15), the only man who was inherently good (2 Corinthians 5:21), the only man who was sinless (2 Corinthians 5:21), the only man who could walk in perfect righteousness (Hebrews 4:15; 1 Peter 2:21-23), and the only man who could "suffer and die" for sinners as a man, though he was God. Jesus rose again, defeating death and sin, for He is God (Hebrews 2:14-15). Jesus came and lived and died and rose from the dead as the God/man so that we could be "good" and "righteous" by standing or being clothed in Jesus' righteousness (Romans 3:21-26; Philippians 3:9; Romans 6:1). Why do bad things happen to good people? The "worst" thing happened to the only "good" person (Jesus Christ) as God poured out His wrath on His Son, Jesus Christ, for our sin.

The New Testament book of Hebrews (Bible), tells us that Jesus learned obedience through the things that He suffered (Hebrews 5:8). If we believe in Jesus we will learn obedience by what we suffer (Hebrews 12:6-7). If we believe in Jesus we will participate in the sufferings of Christ (1 Peter 4:12-13). Suffering shows us that we are weak and that we need a strength that is outside of us (Psalm 61:1-4; Psalm 73:25-26; 1 Peter 4:11). The Bible tells us that Jesus gives strength when we are weak and that is to be desired more than our own strength (2 Corinthians 12:9-10; Philippians 4:11-13). Suffering purifies the unnecessary and sinful things out of the believer's life (1 John 1:9; 1 Peter 4:9). Suffering produces a format for practicing the fruit of the Spirit given to the believer in Jesus Christ (2 Timothy 1:7). We will have more compassion, mercy, and love to demonstrate in our suffering, because we have experienced the compassion, mercy, and love that Jesus Christ has poured out on us.

This is quite different than the preceding views of "Why Do We Suffer?" It is clearly not me-centered. It is definitely Christ-centered (1 Peter 2:19). We do not live for ourselves. Nor do we live to see our selfish desires fulfilled. Jesus desires become our desires and we live in

His love. The love of Jesus flows through us to everyone we touch in our lives. In this way, Jesus Christ is honored and glorified. We cannot touch others with the love of Christ if our suffering is more important than the gravity of Jesus Christ's suffering for us. We are given suffering to learn obedience. Through suffering we learn to trust and rely on the strength and grace of Jesus Christ. We are able to comfort others in their suffering, like we have been comforted. Most importantly, suffering prepares us to be able to bear the weight of the holiness of God when we are "absent from the body and present with the Lord".

It is through the Bible that we see how much we don't deserve, how much we have been given, and how much we are loved in Jesus Christ. And so we ask: "Why not me?" "What do I have that I deserve?" "Do I need to repent of sin in my life?" "What can I thank and praise God for in my suffering?" "What can I use to minister to and comfort others?" "How can I love as I have been loved?" "What is the next faithful step?" "How much has Jesus Christ suffered for me?" And ultimately: "How can Jesus Christ be honored and glorified in my suffering?"

"Not only so, but we also glory in our sufferings, because we know that suffering produces perseverance; perseverance, character, and character,

42

hope. And hope does not put us to shame, because God's love has been poured out into our hearts through the Holy Spirit, who has been given to us" (Romans 5:3-5, NIV).

Finally, it is the weight of the holiness of God that truly drives our focus and responses throughout each area of suffering, whether that suffering is a straw or the crescendo that forces its way into our life with more and more intensity. We need to be constantly reminded of the holiness of God.

"For great is the glory of the Lord" (Psalm 138:5b).

"I am the Lord, that is My name, I will not give My glory to another, Nor my praise to graven images" (Isaiah 42:8; Romans 1:18-23).

"In these last days He has spoken to us in His Son, whom He appointed heir of all things, through whom also He made the world. And He is the radiance of His glory and the exact representation of His nature, and upholds all things by the word of His power" (Hebrews 1:2-3).

"Whether, then, you eat or drink or whatever you do, do all to the glory of God" (I Corinthians 10:31; Romans 15:6; I Peter 4:11).

All that we suffer (if we are a believer in Jesus Christ) is preparation for the "weight" of God's glory. If we are not prepared to be with the Lord in heaven, why would we think we would do well in heaven?

"For momentary, light affliction is producing for us an eternal weight of glory far beyond all comparison, while we look not at the things which are seen, but at the things which are not seen; for the things which are seen are temporal, but the things which are not seen are eternal" (2 Corinthians 4:17-18).

We trust in God's sovereignty, wisdom, power, grace, and great love. It is sufficient in our suffering to display the holiness of God to others. It is sufficient to be satisfied with the worth and weight of God's holiness.

"Thus says the Lord, 'Let not a wise man boast of his wisdom, and let not the mighty man boast of his might, let not a rich man boast of his riches; but let him who boasts boast of this, that he understands and knows Me, that I am the Lord who exercises loving kindness, justice, and righteousness on earth; for I delight in these things,' declares the Lord" (Jeremiah 9:23-24).

"Dear friends, do not be surprised at the fiery ordeal that has come on you to test you, as though something strange were happening to you. But rejoice inasmuch as you participate in the sufferings of Christ, so that you may be overjoyed when his glory is revealed. If you are insulted because of the name of Christ, you are blessed, for the Spirit of glory and of God rests on you. If you suffer, it should not be as a murderer or thief or any other kind of criminal, or even as a meddler. However, if you suffer as a Christian, do not be ashamed, but praise God that you bear that name. For it is time for judgment to begin with the God's household; and if it begins with us, what will the outcome be for those who do not obey the gospel of God? And, 'If it is hard for the righteous to be saved, what will become of the ungodly and the sinner?' So then, those who suffer according to God's will should commit themselves to their faithful Creator and continue to do good" (I Peter 4:12-19, NIV).

"In the multitude of my anxious

thoughts within me--

You Lord,

comfort, cheer and delight my soul."

–See Psalm 94:19

–Peaks and Valleys, Grace Gospel Publishers

CHAPTER 4

A Depiction of Pain

"A happy heart makes the face cheerful,
but heartache crushes the spirit."
—Proverbs 15:13, NIV

"Why is my pain unending
and my wound grievous and incurable?"
—Jeremiah 15:18a, NIV

Suffering in any fashion or form brings pain. Pain, in varying degrees, affects every part of a person. We are not animals. We are created in the image of God (Genesis 1:27). We have the ability to reason, to make decisions, to laugh, to cry, to worry, to feel pain, to feel sadness, to feel stress, to feel joy, to feel exuberance, and we have the need to know God. At the time of our greatest suffering we will be at our weakest. Sleep disturbances will become the normal. Physical strength, mental capacities, and emotional stability are all not operating normally.

Pain Brings Exhaustion

The person who has pain expends their energies throughout the day fighting the physical effects of the pain while trying to accomplish daily tasks. Physical energy that was needed to accomplish such tasks is now divided between fighting the pain and accomplishing those tasks. Weariness, tiredness, and then exhaustion, become a way of life. More and more chores are left undone and extra tasks just don't get done. It just takes too much energy.

The person who has emotional pain will often deal with more exhaustion than the person with physical pain. Emotional pain seems to cut so deep that there is not just weariness, but absolute exhaustion and the inability to make yourself move. Curling up in bed, even in a fetal position, is not abnormal.

Exhaustion dulls mental and spiritual capacities. Thinking, reasoning, talking, and even praying just takes too much effort. Losing the desire to do anything that is above and beyond the normal is typical. Exhaustion can also make one very sensitive emotionally. It will be easy to weep, and sometimes, even easier to throw up one's hands and quit.

Pain Affects a Person Mentally

Exhaustion, emotions, physical weakness, illness, loss, and resulting pain all take its toll on the mind. Forgetfulness, the inability to focus, hearing or listening, difficulty in making decisions, poor judgment, the presence of fear, inability to deal with stress, and issues of faith are all varying affects of living with pain. The mind becomes cloudy as if the one in pain is in a fog. Details become unimportant. Functionality is limited. Each physical step is determined by the agony in the mind. The presence of fear can also cause a person to be irrational and/or make poor decisions. Those who impart fear and prey on the one suffering with their strength can cause even more pain.

Pain Brings Emotional Battles

Pain is not just a harsh sensation but is an emotional experience. Emotions can act very similarly to a roller coaster ride. Within the space of a few seconds or minutes the highs and lows of laughter and weeping may be experienced. Along with the highs and lows come shock, feeling of loss, relief, guilt, frustration, discouragement, helplessness, panic, anxiousness, worry, loss of appetite, loneliness, emptiness, hopelessness, and depression. The volatility of these emotions can be shocking to the one suffering. It feels as if there is no solid foundation and no hope.

Pain Brings Many Struggles In the Spirit

The life that is based on truth, particularly the truth of the Scripture, will be shocked at how faith can be rocked by pain. Having discussed the types of suffering, whether it be the "straw" or the "crescendo", it is noted that faith is not rocked at every straw, but often rocked as the crescendo increases with pain. Questions and answers are searched by the spirit of a person. Guilt and self-torment can create more pain. Self-pity can wreak havoc on the spirit. The realization of wrong doing or sin can bring more mourning. There is often a struggle with hopelessness and lack of purpose. The spirit of a person greatly affects the functionality of the physical body.

Pain Isolates

Isolation is one of the defining elements of pain. Pain causes one to be acutely sensitive to the fact that life has changed. There is no longer the "normal" that exists in others. From dawn to dusk and throughout the night, pain dominates and replaces what was once normal living. Strength is replaced with weakness. Sensitive emotions bring withdrawal. The understanding from others and the common ground with others is found to be almost non-existent. Often the final nail of isolation is accomplished through the rejection of others. Those that feel the depth of isolation are not likely to cry out for help.

Pain Changes a Person

Pain exists to inform that something is wrong. It could be something is wrong with the body such as an injury or an illness. Maybe there are issues with the functionality of the brain. Sometimes the road of pain comes from loss of relationship due to rejection or death. In any case, the one who has pain cannot be expected to be the same person known prior to the incurred pain.

Pain Leaves Scars

Most injuries, upon healing, will leave scars. A broken thumb, broken collarbone, broken ribs, broken hip will all show scars visible on an x-ray. Emotional and mental pain also leaves one with scars. These are not always seen by a visible mark. They may be seen by the change in a person's general mood, disposition, or personality. Scars of any kind, seen or unseen, can bring a soberness or seriousness to life. Pain reminds one of the brevity of life.

Each person has a different level of tolerance to pain. What is considered pain to one person may not be considered pain to another person. Pain is the measure that stretches each person to grow and change. Growth can be defined by bitterness or by walking in hope. True hope can only be found in Jesus Christ.

CHAPTER 5

Let's Talk About Hope

"Where then is my hope?
Who can see any hope for me?"
—Job 17:15, NIV

Hope can be defined in many ways. The intellectual may run to the dictionary and find that hope means:

"A desire of some good, accompanied with or a belief that is obtainable. Hope differs from *wish* and *desire* in this, that it implies some expectation of obtaining the good desired, or the possibility of possessing it. *Hope* therefore always gives pleasure or joy; whereas *wish* and *desire* may produce or be accompanied with pain and anxiety" (© 1967 by Rosalie J. Slater, American Dictionary of the American Language, Noah Webster 1828).

The average person may define hope by the actions and circumstances of their life. Some may define hope by their position in life. Another may define hope by the idea of justice versus injustice. A grieving person may define hope as the ability to walk forward without continual sorrow. The person walking in physical pain may see that hope is gradually achieved as pain subsides. Anyone with loss of possession, relationship, job, limb, health, position, or home may find hope in replacement of that loss or in finding a "new normal". Each of these definitions places the boundaries of hope clearly on something tangible and/or something achieved.

The circumstances and achievement of hope can truly be quite nebulous. Think of the different people known in life and how that "striving" for hope is defined. As I reflect on this, I see the majority of people "striving" for something that is tangible, whether it is a relationship, a thing, an idea, a position, or a lifestyle. Hope, as an idea, is the vehicle that brings joy and pleasure to a person in this life. It is an idea that is foundational in each one of us. Throughout all of life each person is driven and managed by this idea. Hope is the reason we get out of bed in the morning. Hope is the reason we pick up our spoon or fork and put food in our mouth each day. Hope is the reason we work, maintain our home, take care of our bodies, build relationships, seek pleasure, pursue justice, and value morality. Without hope, each one of us would cease to exist with purpose. Ecclesiastes 9:4 says, "Anyone who is among the living has hope—even a live dog is better off than a dead lion!" (NIV)

One of the quickest ways to kill hope in an individual is to take away the very thing, relationship, or purpose on which hope is based. Proverbs 13:12 says, "Hope deferred makes the heart sick, but a longing fulfilled is a tree of life." Job 7:6 says, "My days are swifter than a weaver's shuttle, and they come to an end without hope." Truly, the life blood of the human race lies in this simple four letter word — HOPE.

In order to attain a hope that does not dissipate, we are confronted with a question similar to Chapter 3. Can a steadfast and sure hope be found in something that is tangible and driven by the circumstances of life? If our hope is in relationship and any part of that relationship is tainted by death, illness, or rejection, what then? If our hope is in possession and there is loss of home, finances, belongings, goods, or good name, what then? If our hope is in health or mortality and all is lost, what then? If our hope is in pleasure and this ceases, what then? Is it possible for a thing or an idea to truly bring the fulfillment of hope? If hope is so necessary to life, and the circumstances of life are at times as volatile as emotions can be in grief, then why do we place such a value of hope on "anything" that can dissipate in a moment?

I submit to the reader that this is the foolishness of the human mind and heart which places all of its value on what is temporal and soon to be passing away. This is the reason that the emotion of anger erupts out of suffering, particularly severe suffering. Anger displays the selfishness that is rooted in the human heart. Anger defies the death of what is desired. "I want." "I did not get what I wanted." "My hope is dashed to pieces." "You just don't understand my pain." "My bad is worse than your bad." "I have a right to be angry." Anger calls into question the goodness of God and His providence in each life. Do we have the right to question God's purposes? Do we have the right to be angry?

The only way to maintain "hope" in and through all the changing circumstances of life, regardless of the pleasure or difficulty in life, is to have a "hope" that is secure and never changing. Once again, we find our answer in the God/man, Jesus Christ. Other religions are constantly changing as they are influenced by society, culture, media, and new revelation. "Jesus Christ is the same yesterday and today and forever" (Hebrews 13:8). Jesus is the Son of God and yet equal to God in all power and authority and purity (John 1:1-2; Hebrews 1:3a). God the Father had a plan for God the Son to be born as a man (Luke 2:1-20), to grow and live as a perfect man (though still 100% God), to die for sinners as a perfect man (2 Corinthians 5:21), to be resurrected from the dead showing His power over death as God (1 Peter 1:3), and to return to His place at the right hand of God the Father (Hebrews 1:3b). It is from this place the God/man, Jesus Christ, is continually interceding with understanding, for all those that He purchased with His life and blood when He died and rose again (Hebrews 7:25). Jesus calls us to place our "hope" in Him (Psalm 43:5; Psalm 62:5; Hebrews 6:18). Jesus never changes (Hebrews 13:8). Jesus is our hope for strength when we are weak (Isaiah 40:31). Jesus is our hope for comfort (2 Corinthians 1:7, 10). Jesus is our hope for purpose to go on living in the face of tragic events (Jeremiah 29:11). Jesus is our hope for relationship (1 Thessalonians 2:19). Jesus is our hope for cleansing (Galatians 5:5; I John 3:3). Jesus is our hope for joy and happiness (1 Timothy 6:17). Jesus is our hope for contentment and peace (Romans 15:13). Jesus is our hope for love (Romans 5:5; 1 Corinthians 13:13; Colossians 1:5). Jesus is our hope for the future (Romans 8:25). Jesus is even our hope for our future home (1 Corinthians 15:19; Titus 1:2).

Within each one of us is the desire for some form of security and this security is intertwined with hope. As we place our security in Jesus Christ, we will find unending hope, changeless hope, and hope with a future.

"Such is the destiny of all who forget God; so perishes the <u>hope</u> of the godless" (Job 8:13, NIV).

"You will be secure, because there is <u>hope</u>; you will look about you and take your rest in safety" (Job 11:18, NIV).

"Be strong and take heart, all you who <u>hope</u> in the Lord" (Psalm 31:24, NIV).

"But the eyes of the Lord are on those who fear him, on those whose <u>hope</u> is in his unfailing love" (Psalm 33:18, NIV).

"We wait in <u>hope</u> for the Lord; he is our help and our shield" (Psalm 33:20, NIV).

"But now, Lord, what do I look for? My <u>hope</u> is in you" (Psalm 39:7, NIV).

What is your hope in life and death?

CHAPTER 6

Comfort With Hope

"This is why I weep
and my eyes overflow with tears.
No one is near to comfort me,
No one to restore my spirit."
–Lamentations 1:16a, NIV

When I hear a tragic story that ends in injury or death, my heart jumps out of me and runs toward that person(s). Immediately sadness overwhelms me and sometimes I cannot stop the tears from flowing. Prayer flows from within as I beseech the Lord to show His love and care and provide strength and grace that are needed. I want to run and tell the person who is suffering that God is good and He can be trusted. My door is open to listen when the words come, and tenderness is there when hugs are needed. My sadness is there for many reasons. I understand their agony. I know that their world is forever changed. The emotional struggles, the fragility of the mind, and striving to find their "new normal" are right around the corner. The duration of the suffering is unknown. Each person is "so unique" that determining how to comfort them truly requires the wisdom of God.

There are patterns that take place when an illness, tragedy, or death occurs.

There Is the First Rush of Help.

There are those willing to help with immediate needs by running errands, providing food, helping with the work load, watching children, giving funds, aiding in decisions, and much needed prayer. These acts of love to the suffering one are short in duration and meet the need of the immediate. I call this "Shock Comfort". This comfort is greatly appreciated and necessary, but the one suffering is still suffering.

There Is the Second Rush of Help.

The days and weeks that follow a tragedy are filled with dinner invitations, companionship outings, provision of food, kind words, an occasional hug, greetings (with the request to know how one is doing), and much needed prayer. These acts of love to the suffering one are a little longer than the first rush of help, but in time, this too, ends. I call this "Follow Up Comfort". This comfort is also needed and appreciated, but the one suffering is still suffering.

There is No Third Rush of Help.

The days that follow the ending of the "Follow Up Comfort" are more often than not excruciating. The majority of participants in a tragedy have gone back to their "normal" lives and the suffering one is left to live a life that is no longer the normal once known. A new widow or widower, is now very much alone and that aloneness is felt. If a child is lost, the one suffering is learning to go on without their future. In the face of severe injuries, the injured one is learning how to make it, alone, no matter what the physical condition. If a child is born with defects, the parent(s) begin the arduous task of caring for this child alone. A person used to reoccurring bouts of illness, retains the difficulty of normal living during these bouts of reoccurring illness. The parent with a wayward child, is most likely still mourning a wayward child. If there is one in deep financial trouble, that one is more than likely still having financial trouble. Losing a job, often still leaves one without a job.

Yes (if you are a believer in Jesus Christ), you will struggle and learn to depend on the Lord. Yes (if you are a believer in Jesus Christ), you will grow in faith as you depend on the Lord's strength and grace. And yes, some will still pray for the one suffering, which is needed. I call this "Comfort Still Needed".

Suffering leaves an unresolved problem. The widow or widower is still lonely and needs physical help. The one who lost a child is still in agony. The one with health problems very likely still has health problems, needing physical help. The child with defects still has defects, leaving a parent overly burdened. The one with financial trouble and the one without a job just has more stress (with fear) trying to pay the bills without help. Even when others end their comfort, comfort is still needed.

As you read the first couple of chapters, what were your thoughts? How would you come alongside me and offer comfort and hope? How would you show me love? What would you say to me? What kind of confidence would you offer me in my suffering? Would you have understanding? Would you be able to relate to me? Do you have a confidence in the sovereign providence of God and His truth that would be relayed to me with assurance of the goodness of God? Or, would you encourage me with the right to be angry at God for what has happened not just once but multiple times? What would be your purpose in comforting me? Would you just want my suffering to stop or would you want me to submit to the providence of God in my suffering? Would you encourage me to be thankful in my circumstances? Would you encourage me to bow my knee with submission before the Lord and say with Job, "The Lord gave and the Lord has taken away, blessed be the name of the Lord" (Job 1:21)?

As you read Chapter 4, the physical, mental, and spiritual condition of the one suffering is noted. Suffering is often accentuated by the "straw" or the "crescendo". The one who is suffering can be compared to a person with Alzheimer. No one really desires to have the dreaded disease of Alzheimer, which often comes with age, and yet there is a very strong correlation between the Alzheimer patient and the person who has severe suffering. There is the indication of stress and the emotions that come with stress. Along with that comes difficulty in focusing, remembering, retaining information, thinking, and reasoning. Emotions are volatile and isolation inevitably follows. There truly is no hope of improvement for the person with Alzheimer, but there is hope of attaining a "new normal" for the one suffering.

This hope for a "new normal" must be nourished and encouraged in the person who is suffering by others who are rich in compassion and mercy. The length of suffering should not leave the one suffering in the category of "Comfort Still Needed". Instead, love—which truly must be love flowing from the Lord Jesus through the comforter to the suffering one—will not find the needed comfort to be burdensome but light and a joy to impart.

Standing on the outside looking in on someone who is suffering (like me), is often difficult. It is like seeing someone in a wheelchair at the store, seeing someone in a parking lot that is missing a limb, or seeing someone who is not quite right mentally. There are several responses that often occur. There is embarrassment because it isn't normal. Or one is overcome with emotion and sorrow. Words are difficult to find. The agony in the one suffering is hard to bear. A question may arise as to whether that person deserves that suffering. Other thoughts and fears may surface—"What if that were me?"

Suffering causes a person to stand out as different. Even an Alzheimer patient knows, in their coherent moments, what is happening to them. The blessing of this disease is the forgetfulness that immediately follows. The one suffering does not have this comfort. Instead, the one suffering is assured each moment, of each day, of the agony of change.

It is natural to have expectations and assumptions in regard to other participants in our lives. There are also expectations and assumptions in regard to the fundamental idea of being comforted or comforting another who is suffering. "Shock Comfort" and "Follow Up Comfort" primarily meet immediate needs, as we read earlier. The meeting of these needs is often for the benefit of the comforter as much as for the benefit of the one being comforted. What about when there is "Comfort Still Needed"?

One of the primary objectives of real comfort is the ability to set aside all expectations and assumptions towards the one suffering. In essence, this is putting aside what we would want and how we perceive comfort is needed. It takes Godly wisdom to really know someone. As much as possible, it requires putting oneself in another's shoes, and "listening", really "listening" to the one suffering. It will then be possible to hear their needs. Are they lonely? Did they lose a family member(s)? Are they isolated? Have they lost the person(s) who physically touched them and shared their daily events? Do they eat alone (once they ate with others)? Are they staying in bed until afternoon? Are they able to accomplish daily tasks? Are they able to think? Are they having trouble making decisions? Are they frantic? Are they scared? Are they depressed? Are they crushed and broken? It is so important to listen as they cry for help! Do you see their real needs? What about God? Are they staying away from the means of grace (worship and dwelling on Christ)? Comfort is much more beneficial when it comes with understanding. This includes coming alongside the one suffering without preconceived assumptions.

Once the true state of the person suffering is determined, the primary goal of comfort is to encourage with hope. Hope is the foundation for restoration and encouragement. Hope comes alongside by lending a heart of love until the suffering one is established in their "new normal."

The foundation of hope for all Godly comfort is a vivid understanding of the covenantal faithfulness of God towards His children. He does not give us one chance or two chances or even three chances and then tell us we had our chances. He does give us the promise of His lovingkindness in Isaiah 54:9-10 which says,

"For this is like the days of Noah to Me; when I swore that the waters of Noah should not flood the earth again, so I have sworn that I will not be angry with you, nor will I rebuke you. For the mountains may be removed and the hills may shake, but My lovingkindness will not be removed from you, and My covenant of peace will not be shaken,' says the Lord who has compassion on you."

That lovingkindness is not just a "sent card" or a "wish-you-well" or "just affection" or "simply a commitment" or "a desire only". All of these ideas are all wrapped up together each time His lovingkindness is displayed, and action follows. God is saying that His lovingkindness will NOT be removed. This is God's heart. He doesn't tell us to wait or to get in line or follow steps one, two, and three. This God stoops to our level and speaks to us on our level. He has a heart of compassion, covenantal faithfulness, divine affections and commitment all wrapped up together in His compassion for us. It is so strong that just like the mountains that cannot be removed, His lovingkindness cannot be removed. This is our foundation for comfort and hope.

A Depiction of Lovingkindness

It is time. One friend told me to call her anytime day or night. Another friend made a cup of tea, offered all the time needed to encourage, and offered advice with wisdom and understanding. Another friend also offered time, in addition to sharing the wisdom of God's love, which she also expressed with hugs. This has been huge, now that I am alone. The husbands (also my friends) of all of these friends joined their wives in this thoughtful and wise help. I can still call any of these dear friends at any time for wisdom or help. This is a picture of the lovingkindness of the Lord.

It is listening. True listening is like listening to the Alzheimer patient who says the same thing over and over and the listener hears, each time, as if it were the first time, with gentleness and dignity for the one suffering. This is a picture of the lovingkindness of the Lord.

It is belonging. The parent, son, daughter, brother, sister that values time with and care for the one suffering.

It is the gentle and patient speech of others given to the one suffering. Lovingkindness bears with the broken.

"Gentle words bring life and health; a deceitful tongue crushes the spirit" (Proverbs 15:4, NLT).

It is the gentle touch of a handshake, an arm around the shoulder, a kiss on the cheek, or a tender-hearted hug. Even the Lord holds and carries His suffering children. Words are not always necessary and can often be harmful.

It is constant encouragement to trust in the Lord and His sovereignty.

"We urge you, brethren, admonish the unruly, encourage the fainthearted, help the weak, be patient with everyone" (1 Thessalonians 5:14; Acts 20:34).

It is sending a note from your daily scripture reading to encourage or a card with prayer.

It is eating with others and not just being brought a meal. This is just like the communion and fellowship that we have with the Lord:

"...they were taking their meals together with gladness and sincerity of heart" (Acts 2:46b).

"But if we walk in the Light as He Himself is in the Light, we have fellowship with one another, and the blood of Jesus His Son cleanses us from all sin" (1 John 1:7).

It is coming by to visit and sitting with the one suffering.

"Pure and undefiled religion in the sight of our God and Father is this; to visit orphans and widows in their distress, and to keep oneself unstained by the world" (James 1:27).

It is weeping freely without condemnation.

"You keep track of all my sorrows. You have collected all my tears in your bottle. You have recorded each one in your book" (Psalm 56:8, NLT).

It is relieving burdens that are overwhelming. This means coming alongside and stepping into another's world in order to help with crushing burden. Wise advice without ulterior motives is greatly needed.

"Bear one another's burdens, and thereby fulfill the law of Christ" (Galatians 6:2; Job 26:2; Acts 20:34).

It is not adding burdens. Love does not place one more burden on the person that is suffering and already burdened. This requires current knowledge of the sufferer's condition.

"A bruised reed He will not break and a dimly burning wick He will not extinguish; He will faithfully bring forth justice" (Isaiah 42:3; Matthew 12:20).

It is including the one suffering (who no longer has a family structure) in your family and giving them a sense of belonging. This is huge. As Christians, we have a large family that far surpasses the physical family structure.

It is prayer. To this day I am reminded of an older lady who prays every day for my son and myself. I am humbled by such faithfulness. This is a picture of the lovingkindness of the Lord as He intercedes before the throne of God for the one suffering.

"Who then will condemn us? No one—for Christ Jesus died for us and was raised to life for us, and he is sitting in the place of honor at God's right hand, pleading for us" (Romans 8:34, NLT).

Comfort with hope is all wrapped up in lovingkindness that leaves the one suffering with compassion and dignity.

"The soothing tongue

is a tree of life,

but a perverse tongue crushes the spirit."

–Proverbs 15:4, NIV

"Again, I [the Teacher] observed

all the oppression

that takes place under the sun.

I saw the tears of the oppressed,

with no one to comfort them.

The oppressors have great power,

and their victims are helpless."

–Ecclesiastes 4:1, NLT

CHAPTER 7

You Did What?

Time stretches endlessly before the one suffering. Pain makes the one suffering acutely sensitive to everything. Strength has now become weakness. At times the pain can be so encompassing that the one suffering may fail to recognize the depth of God's love in the midst of these providential circumstances. There is deep vulnerability in the one suffering. It is in this condition that others will meet the one suffering with a comfort of ignorance, a comfort of compassion, or a comfort of oppression.

Not every person who walks through suffering comes out on the other side with a heart full of compassion for those that suffer. In many cases, suffering brings about the hardening of the heart and the preservation of "self" is more important than compassion. In the animal kingdom we call this "survival of the fittest". I have raised chickens for many years. If a chicken has a sore spot or is wounded, the other chickens will peck continuously on that spot or wound until they eventually kill the weaker chicken. This is seen throughout all species of creatures.

Sadly, even people who are created in the image of God, with the moral attributes of God, will act like creatures that do not show these moral attributes, in their desire for "self" preservation.

When tragedy strikes, the "Ripple Affect" occurs. First, there is a large splash when a tragic event or circumstance brings initial loss and pain. The large splash can be loss of family member(s), injury, terminal diagnosis, financial devastation, etc. All of the little ripples that expand from the large splash continue to bring ripples of pain. These smaller ripples can be loss of other relationships, body parts, good health, time, belongings, home, future, etc. Extending past the prior ripples can often be the ripple of oppression.

Chapter 4 reminds us of the physical, mental, and spiritual condition of the one who is in pain.

➢ Pain dominates waking and sleeping hours.
➢ Pain is exhausting.
➢ Pain makes it difficult to really rest.
➢ Pain can make it difficult to concentrate and think.
➢ Pain affects memory retention.
➢ Pain impacts decision making.
➢ Pain causes a volatility of emotions.
➢ Pain may cause depression.

- Pain may influence physical health.
- Pain permeates relationships.
- Pain determines the value of "true" friends.
- Pain isolates.
- Pain may cause one to question God and His truth.
- Pain challenges the purpose of life.
- Pain may cause a feeling of being lost.
- Pain may influence one's desire to live.
- Pain strikes at the very core of thankfulness.

It is obvious, from this list of difficulties that flow out of pain, the one suffering is in dire need of "true" compassion. It is also noted that the one suffering is a prime target for those who will exploit the weakness and suffering of the one in pain.

It is not always easy to assess the motives and character of another. Often it takes particular circumstances and time to bring to light the propensities in motives and character. Either you will see genuine, consistent compassion with concern for the one suffering which flows out of a changed heart or you will see oppressive comfort with concern for the good of the comforter which flows out of a hardness of heart. One heart follows God and the other heart follows self. Humility, gratitude, dependence on Christ, and contrition are all characteristic attitudes of the truly converted; the basis out of which Christians experience joy and love. When the gospel truly does its work "proud Christian" is an unthinkable absurdity. Instead the gospel is demonstrated in self-humiliation and God glorified.

Oppressive comfort does not always start out this way. In the early days of comfort there may be a seeming genuine kindness. In time, it could be that pride, jealousy, greed or all of them rear their head. It is difficult for a strong person to stand against these horrible attitudes, let alone a person who is suffering and weak.

We all have relationships in our lives. There are mothers, fathers, brothers, sisters, aunts, uncles, cousins, husband, wife, friends, coworkers, business associates, and so on. Often, the one suffering—if they even have the strength—will need to be the most careful with people they already know. Sometimes, carefulness needs to be cultivated in regard to others in the church or the work place. Not every person's public and private face is the same. The one suffering needs warnings that will keep them from further pain—if they are not too weak to hear. The one comforting needs to consider warnings that will help them guard against producing further pain in one that is suffering.

Well-Meaning

- ➢ Think about what you say to the suffering one.
- ➢ Do you overwhelm the one suffering with questions (i.e. interrogate)?
    - Do you ask thoughtless questions or make statements that crush the one suffering?
    - Everything will be okay.
    - How are you doing?
    - Do you need anything?
    - Are you still sad?
    - Don't cry!
    - I know exactly how you feel.
    - It is better this way.
    - You have to hold up.
    - Are you doing okay financially?
    - Just let me know if you need anything.
    - I understand what you are going through (when you don't).
    - You must be strong now.
    - You'll get over it.
    - Are you going to have more children?
    - Do you think you will remarry?
    - You are still young; you can remarry and have another child.
    - It is time to put this behind you now.

- At least he didn't suffer.
- Time heals all wounds.
- Call me if you need anything.
- You shouldn't feel that way.
- You'll get through it, just be strong.
- He/She is in a better place.
- This is God's will.
- It's been awhile, aren't you over it yet?
- Everything happens for a reason, life goes on.

➤ Do you offer free advice without really knowing the one suffering?

➤ Do you listen to what the one suffering is really saying?

➤ Are you looking past the surface of what is said to hear, really hear, what is being said?

➤ Do you encourage relationship with others that you only know publicly? Are you <u>sure</u> that the person you are recommending has a public and private face that is the same?

➤ Do you keep in mind that generally the one suffering will privatize feelings, concerns, and affairs? In other words, they are not necessarily going to share how they are really doing. Pain not only isolates and assumes that others do not truly understand, but also brings an inability to express how they are really doing.

Many of you who are reading this would not even think of acting in the following manners. But it does happen, usually behind the scene or under cover, where the oppressive comforter thinks no one sees. Sometimes the oppressive comforter even demands that the one suffering speaks to no one about what is really going on behind the scene. In extreme cases, the oppressive comforter may even threaten the life of the one suffering if this oppressive behavior is exposed.

Expectations and Assumptions

➤ Expecting the one suffering to have the same abilities and capabilities as they have had in the past.

➤ Expecting the one suffering to want a challenge on top of the burdens they already carry. They do not need a challenge, another burden to carry.

➤ Adding another burden can be insurmountable and bring the one suffering into depression.

➤ Assuming that the one suffering needs more to do with no consideration for what is already on their plate or capabilities that are present in the state of pain.

> Assuming that someone with poor health or someone that is very old can just go get a job and work, when their funds have not been handled wisely.

> Expectation of friendship when the one suffering may have a sudden windfall of money.

> Assuming that the one suffering does not need help or friends even though they are destitute financially and relationally. Clearly there is no understanding of the fear of not being able to pay one's bills or the need for companionship.

> Assuming that the person is just fine, from outward appearances, without taking the time to walk beside someone and really find out their circumstances. Their circumstances are usually not what one might think. Quite often their circumstances are more difficult than assumed.

> Expecting obedience from the one suffering instead of giving the one suffering comfort.

> Expecting the one suffering to meet the needs of the comforter whether they are financial, relational, or help oriented.

- Expecting to use the resources of the one suffering for the comforter's own gain while helping the one suffering. In the process, the comforter is hindering the one suffering from being able to maintain their affairs, while the comforter's affairs are maintained.
- Expecting the one suffering to meet the comforter's needs in a better way than the comforter would meet their own needs or wants.
- Taking more from the one suffering than is being given by the one who is suffering.
- Expecting certain time limits on grieving or pain.

Exploit the Weakness and Suffering of Others
- Helping the one suffering with the expectation of gaining monetarily from the funds of the one suffering. This could be undertaking a hired job for the one suffering with the anticipation of gaining more than was agreed upon, treating the one suffering like they are your bank, expecting the one suffering to pay for everything, and so on. If anger is expressed when this expectation is addressed, the assessment has been accurate.

➤ Insisting on the help of the one suffering, generally at the expense of things the one suffering needs to do, with promises of help that are never kept.

➤ Providing a service that is not done well with the expectation of payment for a job done well.

➤ Making decisions for the one suffering that benefit the comforter and not the one suffering.

➤ Destruction of property belonging to the one suffering with no intention of making it right.

➤ Owing money to the one suffering with no intention of paying your debt. This can be the very lifeline the one suffering needs to meet their financial responsibilities.

➤ Divide and conquer family relationships so that the one comforting has the weak, suffering one in their grip and under their control.

➤ Alienate the one suffering from family relationships so that one can end relationship with the dead spouse's family, cut off relationship with living children, cease relationship with extended family, halt relationship with the comforter's family that the one suffering sees regularly, and so on. Generally this alienation is for some benefit that the one comforting derives from the one suffering.

➤ Profess ownership of another human being. This can be displayed in dictating someone's time, abilities, belongings, and loyalty.

Demoralization Instead of Encouragement

➤ Destroying the confidence of the one suffering by constantly putting them down. It could be a mix of both lifting up and putting down the one suffering that destroys confidence.

➤ Encouraging the one suffering to do something that they are not capable of doing at this time. This just dumps more on the one who is suffering which can crush instead of encourage.

➤ Telling the one suffering they just need to get over it is harsh and abusive.

➤ Telling the one suffering they don't listen is cold-hearted.

➤ Endeavoring to control the very words of the one suffering.

➤ Telling the one suffering that they will never get the mess in their life fixed is brutal.

➤ Condemning speech when memories of loved ones are shared is like being punched in the gut.

Often the person with such behavior will reserve for themselves the right to speak of memories even though they have negated this in the one suffering.

➤ Pressure to immediately get rid of the belongings of a loved one.

➤ Belittling the person who is dead crushes the one who is grieving.

➤ Yelling and screaming profanities at the one who is suffering.

➤ Imposing a lack of morality in one's conversations.

➤ Lying to and about others with defense of the lies. The lies, of course, being advantageous to the one comforting.

➤ Using affection as a weapon.

➤ Hindering the one suffering from comforting another one who is suffering.

➤ Making fun of someone or the one suffering in order to influence their decision making.

➤ The comforter imposes their own fears with force on the one suffering. The person who puts fear or doubt regarding a subject in front of the one suffering may not realize how that is magnified within the one suffering. Fear can cause one to be irrational and make poor decisions. Those who impart fear and prey on the one suffering with their strength can cause great damage to the one who is suffering.

➢ Treating the one suffering with no mercy.

➢ Treating the one suffering with a lack of dignity.

➢ Treating the one suffering like a dog that can be kicked off whenever one desires.

➢ Professing to know God and yet having little or no display of His love in patience, gentleness, kindness, selflessness, and self-control towards the one suffering.

God <u>is</u> redeeming and restoring a fallen, broken people into the likeness of His Son, Jesus Christ, for His own glory! Our walk in suffering and our walk in comfort of others, by His grace, should cause other people to come to the right conclusions about God. As people created in the image of God, we are called to praise and to bring honor to God in all circumstances and all relationships of life. What a privilege to be used of God in this way, knowing it is His power doing it!

"But our bodies have many parts, and God has put each part just where he wants it. How strange a body would be if it had only one part! Yes, there are many parts, but only one body. The eye can never say to the hand, 'I don't need you.' The head can't say to the feet, 'I don't need you.' In fact, some parts of the body that seem weakest and least important are actually the most necessary. And the parts we regard as less honorable are those we clothe with the greatest care. So we carefully protect those parts that should not be seen, while the more honorable parts do not require this special care. So God has put the body together such that extra honor and care are given to those parts that have less dignity. This makes for harmony among the members, so that all the members care for each other. If one part suffers, all the parts suffer with it, and if one part is honored, all the parts are glad" (I Corinthians 12:18-26, NLT).

CHAPTER 8

The Companions You Keep

"You have taken from me
friend and neighbor—
darkness is my closest friend."
—Psalm 88:18, NIV

"One who has unreliable friends
soon comes to ruin,
but there is a friend who
sticks closer than a brother."
—Proverbs 18:24, NIV

If we have everything that we could want, but we don't have relationship (someone to share with), we have nothing. If we have relationship (someone to share with), but are poor in material goods, we have everything. I propose that having true and real relationship with others makes life worth living. Anything appears possible with good relationship.

Relationship may take many forms. A sister calls a brother to chat. Starbucks is the meeting place of two friends for a coffee and a talk. The phone rings and a mother will cherish her son's call. A husband and wife sit closely on the couch while watching a movie. A mother-in-law enjoys lunch with her daughter-in-law. Two brothers enjoy a ball game. A dad helps his son fix a plumbing problem. Friends visit another friend who is house bound. Daughters fix a surprise meal for their parents. Brothers get together and roof a house. A daughter emails her mother with exciting news. Shopping with a couple of friends is a joyful event. An anniversary is celebrated with friends and a special dinner. Cousins enjoy an evening out on the town. A parent may read regularly to a child. And on we could go with all of the ways that relationship is displayed.

These many forms of relationship may also be defined as a family member, a spouse, a friend, a neighbor, or a companion. All of these categories demonstrate some type of walking together. I like the term companion for it describes relationship concisely.

A companion is "one who keeps company with another; one with whom a person frequently associates, and converses" (©1967 by Rosalie J. Slater, American Dictionary of the English Language, Noah Webster 1828).

Companions are acquired through birth into a family, by marriage, through mutual circumstances, by befriending another person, and the unexpected connection of two souls. A companion may also be thrust upon one person by another person. Influence is one of the greatest gifts that a companion gives to his/her companion. Walking with another person in any type of good relationship consists of integrity, selflessness, honesty (trustworthy), morality (virtuous behavior), inoffensiveness, real communication, support, refreshment, and the safeguarding of one another. The quality of one's companions will largely define the quality of one's life.

There are bad companions and good companions. A bad companion has the over-arching principle of self-interest. This can be displayed by moral corruption, greed, habitual lying, stealing, jealousy, judging, gossiping, and/or use of anger. There may also be the pretence of relationship to cause a "companion" to be one's tool in order to get something accomplished that serves the pretender. Selfish people hurt people. Their "self-interest" is above anyone else and automatically blinds the selfish person to what is going on in another's life. Selfish people often go farther in their self-interest and take advantage of whatever is available to them in their "companion's" life, i.e. whatever will benefit them. The selfish person will use whatever means possible to please themselves over and above the interests of their "companion". Sometimes this is called a "backstabber". They will use guilt, bribery, flattery, manipulation, lying, condemnation, intolerance, control, anger and/or cursing to meet their own desires. Truly they display a lack of conscience.

"As for my companion, he betrayed his friends; he broke his promises. His words are as smooth as butter, but in his heart is war. His words are as soothing as lotion, but underneath are daggers" (Psalm 55:20-22, NLT)!

The Old Testament book of Proverbs has many warnings related to companions. Discretion and understanding are a guard against the selfish person who speaks perversely, delights in doing wrong, speaks with flattery, is devious and treacherous, and/or is full of anger. Hurting and abusing another is not part of a good relationship. The reader is warned not to walk with someone who hurts others for their own gain. "My son, do not walk in the way with them. Keep your feet from their path" (Proverbs 1:15). Disobedience to these instructions is like having a wrecking ball crash through one's life.

Bad Companion Checklist

- ➤ Is companionship two-sided or one-sided?
- ➤ Is my companion one way in private and another way in public?
- ➤ Is my companion always bossing me around?
- ➤ Is my companion manipulative and always trying to make me do things I don't want to do?
- ➤ Is my companion bullying someone else or me?
- ➤ Is my companion always judging me?
- ➤ Is my companion always condemning me for something?
- ➤ Is my companion treating me with a lack of dignity?
- ➤ Is my companion habitually telling lies?
- ➤ Is my companion always right?
- ➤ Is my companion always irritable with me?
- ➤ Is my companion angry at me daily?
- ➤ Is my companion greedy regarding what belongs to me?
- ➤ Is my companion spreading rumors about me?
- ➤ Is my companion jealous of praise that others give me?
- ➤ Is my companion mean to me?

Waking up in the morning to a "normal" day that ends with "normal" being replaced by a horrific tragedy will clarify or define the true character of one's companions. When all is well and there are no bumps in the road, a companion's selfishness may be imperceptible or not seen. When all is well, one companion may be investing in a relationship more than another companion with only minimal side affect. When tragedy occurs, the safeguarding of a good companion will be clearly seen. Tragedy will not be the means to take advantage of the companion who is suffering. Instead there will be caring responsebility that nourishes and meets the one in need. A true companion will continue to treat the suffering companion with dignity and will endeavor to help the suffering companion leave their despair sooner; whereas, the bad companion, will find means to fund their own ego at the expense of the companion who is suffering.

True companions walk beside you through thick and thin, they speak the truth in love, they overlook transgressions, they are not only concerned about their own needs or wants or desires, they don't walk away after they get what they want, they are willing to work through difficulties, and they safeguard a friend, sometimes even to their own hurt. A true companion is rooted in Christ and walks as Christ walked in lovingkindness. Truly,

"Love is patient and kind. Love is not jealous or boastful or proud or rude. Love does not demand its own way. Love is not irritable, and it keeps no record of when it has been wronged. It is never glad about injustice but rejoices whenever the truth wins out. Love never gives up, never loses faith, is always hopeful, and endures through every circumstance. Love will last forever..." (I Corinthians 13:4-8a, NLT).

This is how we are loved by God.

One of the greatest displays of a healthy relationship is given to us in the Sermon on the Mount in Matthew 5. It is assumed that any person cannot truly have a healthy relationship with another person unless there is first a healthy relationship with Jesus.

"One day as the crowds were gathering, Jesus went up the mountainside with his disciples and sat down to teach them. This is what he taught them: 'God blesses those who realize their need for him, for the Kingdom of Heaven is given to them. God blesses those who mourn, for they will be comforted. God blesses those who are gentle and lowly, for the whole earth will belong to them. God blesses those who are hungry and thirst for justice, for they will receive it in full. God blesses those who are merciful, for they will be shown mercy. God blesses those whose hearts are pure, for they will see God. God blesses those who work for peace, for they will be called the children of God. God blesses those who are persecuted because they live for God, for the Kingdom of Heaven is theirs. God blesses you when you are mocked and persecuted and lied about because you are my followers. Be happy about it! Be very glad! For a great reward awaits you in heaven. And remember, the ancient prophets were persecuted, too. You are the salt of the earth. But what good is salt if it has lost its flavor? Can you make it useful again? It will be thrown out and trampled underfoot as worthless. You are the light of the world—like a city on a mountain, glowing in the night for all to see. Don't hide your light under a basket! Instead, put it on a stand and let it shine for all. In the same way, let your good deeds shine out for all to see, so that everyone will praise your heavenly Father. Don't misunderstand why I have come. I did not come to abolish the law of Moses or the writings of the prophets. No, I came to fulfill them. I assure you, until heaven and earth disappear, even the smallest detail of God's law will remain until its purpose is achieved. So if you break the smallest commandment and teach others to do the same, you will be the least in the Kingdom of Heaven. But anyone who obeys God's laws and teaches them will be great in the Kingdom of Heaven. But I warn you—unless you obey God better than the teachers of religious law and the Pharisees do, you can't enter the Kingdom of Heaven at all! You have heard that the law of Moses says, 'Do not murder. If you commit murder, you are subject to judgment.' But I say, if you are angry with someone, you are subject to judgment! If you call someone an idiot, you are in danger of being brought before the high council. And if you curse someone, you are in danger of the fires of hell. So if you are standing before the altar in the Temple, offering a sacrifice to God, and you suddenly remember that someone has something against you, leave your sacrifice there beside the altar. Go and be reconciled to that person. Then come and offer your sacrifice to God. Come to terms quickly with your enemy before it is too late and you are dragged into court, handed over to an officer, and thrown in jail. I assure you that you won't be free again until you have paid the last penny. You have heard the law of Moses that says, 'Do not commit adultery.' But I say, anyone who even looks at a woman with lust in his eye has already committed adultery with her in his heart. So if your eye—even if it is your good eye—causes you to lust, gouge it out and throw it away. It is better for you to lose one part of your body than for your whole body to be thrown into hell. And if your hand—even if it is your stronger hand—causes you to sin, cut it off and throw it away. It is better for you to lose one part of your body than for your whole body to be thrown into hell. You have heard that the law of Moses says, 'A man can divorce his wife by merely giving her a letter of divorce.' But I say that man who divorces his wife, unless she has been unfaithful, causes her to commit adultery. And anyone who marries a divorced woman commits adultery. Again, you have heard that the law of Moses says, 'Do not break the vows you have made to the Lord.' But I say, don't make any vows! If you say, 'By heaven!' it is a sacred vow because heaven is God's throne. And if you say, 'By the earth!' it is a sacred vow because the earth is His footstool. And don't swear, 'By Jerusalem!' for Jerusalem is the city of the great King. Don't even swear, 'By my head!' for you can't turn one hair white or black. Just say a simple, 'Yes, I will,' or 'No, I won't.' Your word is enough. To strengthen your promise with a vow shows that something is wrong. You have heard that the law of Moses says, 'If an eye is injured, injure the eye of the person who did it. If a tooth gets knocked out, knock out the tooth of the person who did it.' But I say, don't resist an evil person! If you are slapped on the right cheek, turn the other, too. If you are ordered to court and your shirt is taken from you, give your coat, too. If a soldier demands that you carry his gear for a mile, carry it for two miles. Give to those who ask, and don't turn away from those who borrow. You have heard that the law of Moses says, 'Love your neighbor and hate your enemy.' But I saw, love your enemies! Pray for those who persecute you! In that way, you will be acting as true children of your Father in heaven. For he gives his sunlight to both the evil and the good, and he sends rain on the just and on the unjust, too. If you love only those who love you, what good is that? Even corrupt tax collectors do that much. If you are kind only to your friends, how are you different from anyone else! Even pagans do that. But you are to be perfect, even as your Father in heaven is perfect'" (Matthew 5, NLT).

There is a clear principle taught throughout the Bible regarding a person's speech and a person's actions. Both actions and speech tell everyone acquainted with that person the condition of their heart.

"The good man out of the good treasure of his heart brings forth what is good; and the evil man out of the evil treasure brings forth what is evil; for his mouth speaks from that which fills his heart" (Luke 6:45).

"But the things that proceed out of the mouth come from the heart, and those defile the man. For from the heart come evil thoughts, murder, adultery, all other sexual immorality, theft, lying, and slander" (Matthew 15:18, 19).

If you are at a vulnerable, weak time of your life, take care through prayer that you do not get sucked into a deceptive, destructive relationship. If this warning is too late, then learn from the experience of such a relationship for your own growth and give a warning to others. There is a rather large difference between a true companion and a false companion. Friendship of any kind takes time. Those that claim to be your companion and walk away (lost friends), were never your friends in the first place.

Let those fade out of your life who are not worth keeping. Keep the TRUE companion. There will always be the curious who are just fair weather companions. Sadly, there are also those who pretend to be true but in reality are "wolves in sheep's clothing".

Signs of a Corrupted Heart
- Having a taste for dirty jokes, sexy movies, lies, juicy tidbits of gossip
- Talking to others about someone's private matters
- Laughing at someone instead of with someone
- Attitude of greed, jealousy, hatred
- Seeking the praise of others
- Readiness to tell of other's faults, slander
- Harsh treatment of others
- Talk of getting even or purposeful revenge
- Habit of giving others a piece of one's mind
- Habitual outbursts of anger
- Doesn't listen
- No heart for wisdom
- Always scheming
- Evident selfishness
- No consistency, constantly changing
- Captivated by food, drink, sleep, or sex

➢ Independent spirit that does not submit to authority
➢ Spirit of pride that is always right and never happy
➢ Perpetual cynicism

According to Matthew 5, every relationship is composed of five areas: How to treat others, to judge or not to judge, to condemn or not to condemn, to forgive or not to forgive, and to give or not to give. A healthy relationship with Jesus not only directly influences the companions you walk with, but also influences the way you respond to those that treat you with oppression. Actions quite often speak louder than words.

What kind of companions do you have?

******

"But that isn't what you learned about Christ. Since you have heard about Jesus and have learned the truth that comes from him, throw off your old sinful nature and your former way of life, which is corrupted by lust and deception. Instead, let the Spirit renew your thoughts and attitudes. Put on your new nature, created to be like God—truly righteous and holy. So stop telling lies. Let us tell our neighbors the truth, for we are all parts of the same body. And don't sin by letting anger control you. Don't let the sun go down while you are still angry, for anger gives a foothold to the devil. If you are a thief, quit stealing. Instead, use your hands for good hard work, and then give generously to others in need. Don't use foul or abusive language. Let everything you say be good and helpful, so that your words will be an encouragement to those who hear them. And do not bring sorrow to God's Holy Spirit by the way you live. Remember, he has identified you as his own, guaranteeing that you will be saved on the day of redemption. Get rid of all bitterness, rage, anger, harsh words, and slander, as well as all types of evil behavior. Instead, be kind to one another, just as God through Christ has forgiven you" (Ephesians 4:25-32, NLT).

"Your rulers are rebels, partners with thieves

they all love bribes and chase after gifts.

They do not defend the cause of the fatherless;

the widow's case does not come before them."

–Isaiah 1:23, NIV

CHAPTER 9

What Is True Religion?

"Pure and undefiled religion
in the sight of our God and Father is this:
to visit orphans and widows in their distress,
and to keep oneself unstained by the world."
—James 1:27

People in all walks of life endeavor to find and serve a god they can tolerate and understand. The god they create either provides them with great "blessing" for walking a certain course through life or is very harsh and quick to judge if certain rules are not kept to perfection. Sometimes the god who is created is a combination of both blessing and judgment. The distinction between man's god and the "true" God lies in the great compasssion and overwhelming mercy of the "true" God for the defenseless. God is not a created being in the mind of man. God is and was and always has been. The heart of this God is displayed in these words:

"Pure and undefiled religion in the sight of our God and Father is this: to visit orphans and widows in their distress, and to keep oneself unstained by the world" (James 1:27).

The purity that people long for in the depths of their being, flows out of worship and adoration of the one "true" God. This worship is reflected in the aid and visitation of these two categories of people (orphans and widows) who have not only been left alone, but are defenseless in their distress. If we are worshiping the one "true" God and serving the defenseless with compassion, we are not being influenced or hindered by the philosophies and pleasures of the world.

The word "distress" encompasses the meaning of several words in describing the person who is suffering in pain or anguish. It means affliction, sorrow, agony, grief, misery, ache, pangs, torment, concern, fear, stress, anxiety, difficulty, misfortune, hardship, trial, trouble, and danger. All of these words flow out of being left alone physically. God takes every action by others—good or bad—towards the fatherless and the widows very seriously. God, Himself, becomes the father to the fatherless and the husband to the widow.

"A father to the fatherless, a defender of widows, is God in His holy dwelling" (Psalm 68:5, NIV).

"Do not be afraid; you will not be put to shame. Do not fear disgrace; you will not be humiliated. You will forget the shame of your youth and remember no more the reproach of your widowhood. For your Maker is your husband—the Lord Almighty is his name—the Holy One of Israel is your Redeemer; he is called the God of all the earth" (Isaiah 54:4-5, NIV).

God, Himself, defends the widow and the fatherless.

"He executes justice for the orphan and the widow" (Deuteronomy 10:18a).

No woman or child ever intends to become an orphan or a widow. Most of us have hopes and dreams for our lives that do not include being left alone. But, often, in His providence, God has a better plan, a good plan. Not only does He show us His heart of tenderness towards those that are helpless, but He also displays His glory as He cares for those that are defenseless. The call to true religion—worship and compassion—calls us out of our lives of self-interest and calls us to live for others who are defenseless, as unto the Lord God.

The greatest part of loss is "loving and being loved". Loss can bring out the best and worst in human character. When we look at the picture in James 1:27 of true religion, we see a picture of love. Visiting the orphans and the widows demonstrates how we step outside of our comfort zone to spend time with those that need love, particularly a picture of the love of Christ. While we are spending time with the orphan and the widow we can gain a better understanding of their needs, which will enable us to help meet their needs. Many needs arise out of being left alone. There is the need of companionship, the need of food/shelter without stress, the need of a listening ear, the need of true wisdom, and the need of arms of love that offer comfort. Another avenue of bringing the love of the Lord to them in a physical way is not only stepping into their life, but bringing them into our own home and our family. In these ways, the need for Christ is brought to the one in distress through human care. The essence of true religion is a demonstration of the love of Christ. We are leaving our comfort zone in order to give comfort, in many forms, to those who have little or no physical comfort.

How many times do we walk into a church and hear about the latest program, a small group gathering of some type, missionaries scattered throughout the world, or the messy lives of people in the church? How often do we walk into church and hear a plea to rally around the widows and the orphans in our lives and make them a part of our daily lives? Could this be one of the weakest areas of the church today?

I do not believe that we need one more program in the church today. What we do need is clear Biblical teaching regarding the care of orphans. When we think of orphans, there comes the immediate picture of a child or children who no longer have the love and nourishment of parents (fatherless) or home. The church is one large family composed of individual family units. The body of Christ is compared to a physical body with all of its parts (head, hands, arms, legs, feet, toes, etc.). These orphans and widows are a part of this body and they need help from other parts of this body. The world stresses the philosophy that it is "my four and no more". In other words, we have a Dad, Mom, and the two desired children with no room for more. Children are described in the Word of God as a "blessing". If our homes are ruled by the love of Christ, then the boundaries of our homes can be stretched to include the orphan. The heart of God is described above in James 1:27. Should not our hearts be a reflection of the Lord's heart? Why are we not running to bring orphans into our homes?

In the same context, there is a similar way of caring for the widows. It is interesting that the Bible does not clearly dictate that the church should take care of a "true" widow until she is,

> "not less than sixty years old, having been the wife of one man, having a reputation for good works; and if she has brought up children, if she has shown hospitality to strangers, if she has washed the saints' feet, if she has assisted those in distress, and if she has devoted herself to every good work" (I Timothy 5:9-10).

This limits very concisely the category of widows helped by the church. The challenge to the body of Christ is that we, as members, are given the responsibility of caring for the majority of widows. Any widow that has a child or children or grandchildren should first be cared for by them (I Timothy 5:4). Children or grandchildren that do not care for their mother or grandmother have denied their faith and become worse than an unbeliever (I Timothy 5:8). If the widow is not cared for, then another believing woman is to take on the care of the widow (I Timothy 5:16). This does not leave the care of the widow, younger than sixty, to the church as a program or the deacons as a ministry, but it leaves the care of the widow, younger than sixty, to those who participate in her life.

I propose a radical renovation of the way the church views and cares for the orphans and the widows. The love of Christ calls us to stretch the boundaries of our homes and bring into our family structure those that are defenseless and needing the love of home and family. Each of us has a sphere of people in our lives and a spectrum of people on the edge of that sphere. This is where we start. Which of these people is in need of our home and family? Which of these people is struggling alone to meet emotional and financial stresses? Have we really stepped into the world of any of these people to find out their condition emotionally and financially?

When a child loses parents and a woman loses a husband, they have immediately lost their source of physical protection and love. Emotions that were in the background prior to death are now in the forefront. Fear and inability are huge enemies of the orphan and the widow. Great loss is already realized. There is fear of what they don't know. What of the orphan who just lost his/her security in life? Maybe the widow is fearful of making decisions or making wrong decisions. There could be an inability to pay bills which are mounting with no job or help in sight. It is easy to tell someone to get a job. What if they are emotionally or physically incapable of working at this time? What if they've been a wife and mother and have no qualifications? Those that prey on the defenseless seem to come out of the woodwork. These people can often be friends and family that are the closest to the orphan or widow. They proceed with the "assumptions" that they have, and not on the real facts, concerning the one who is left alone. These people can cause great devastation to the orphan or widow as they satisfy their own self-interest.

There are several examples that come to mind in regard to widows that are taken advantage (hope crushed) of or given an advantage (hope given) now that their physical protector is gone:

> Another year, another winter and the furnace is still not working. An old friend comes by and offers to take a look. The friend ends up spending three hours or more in the attic. When he comes down from the attic, he discusses the problem with the furnace, explains the fix, and

refuses any payment. Instead, he offers the gladness of being able to do this for the widow.

> It is tax time again. The second year in a row, the widow receives a large bill for having her taxes done. Besides that, a mistake made by the tax preparer, compounded from the first year, ends up costing her hundreds of dollars. If her husband were still alive, she would not have been overcharged. He is gone. The tax preparer demonstrates his greed as he takes advantage of the widow. If he had true compassion for the widow, he would have refunded his service fee, after making such an astounding error.

> A young fellow, in the middle of working on his masters in electrical engineering, steps into the life of a young widow and gives her hours and hours of his time and skill to help her finish a seemingly insurmountable task of home construction. Time after time, his faithfulness and kindness was noted and deeply appreciated.

> An older widow has tree work done. Although she was charged a reduced rate with great kindness, I wonder why she was charged at all. Her

provider has passed away. Should not the body of Christ, in the name of Christ, step in and provide the service with full compassion.

- ➤ The Old Testament tells us how the widow was provided with food. Those who grew crops always left some of the crops for those who had no provider. There was no charge for this food. The service was full compassion.

- ➤ There are those that give financial advice to widows with the intent of gleaning some of the widow's money for their own needs or wants.

- ➤ Another widow needed thousands of dollars of tree work done. A lumberjack, with great compassion, hauled off a logging truck full of trees and chipped up a large pile of limbs to mitigate the cost.

- ➤ A man, working for a widow, expects her to be his bank and meet the needs of his family, before his work is performed.

- ➤ A heavy equipment owner provides hours of bobcat work with the refusal of any amount of normal payment.

➤ An older widow finds out a "trusted" family member has been living off of and spending the money the Lord has provided for her livelihood. She now does not have enough to live on the rest of her life. The Lord has taken the life of the "trusted" family member.

➤ A bereaved widow's affairs were taken care of by her lawyer over a lengthy period of time. When asked the amount due, there was nothing due. The service was full compassion.

➤ A fellow withholds payment from a widow which leaves her in financial hardship.

➤ A family member gives time and labor to help a widow with a needed building project.

➤ An acquaintance gives to a widow while taking more than is given.

➤ A neighbor consistently provides readily available help for a widow, since the beginning of widowhood.

➢ A family member refuses to help a widow with her needs.

➢ A young fellow and his family drew a young widow and her family into the security and care of his family. This compassion began and is continuing through the years.

Each participant in the body of Christ is a "manager" of God's resources. I propose that those with valid businesses and services, needed by the widow, retain some of their time and work for the widow in their off work time, very much like crops left in the field for the widow in the Old Testament. Those that have others working for them can also ask them if they would like to donate their time for the business or service needed by the widow. Most people will charge a widow at least something. Many times the quality of the work done for the widow is reprehensible and provides more expenditure for the widow to have the poorly done job rectified.

I also propose, that the widow who has sufficient funds provided for her, have the character to offer payment for services rendered in order to help the giver. Let the widow who has funds also help other widows with their needs as God leads and gives wisdom.

The premise of managing God's resources is based on an attitude of giving and helping. Throughout this attitude is discernment which deters "greed" and "taking advantage". Both the giver and the recipient bear the responsibility of a clear conscience in managing God's resources.

There is a constant tension between self-examination in the light of Biblical truth and rationalization in the light of our own thinking! We need money to care for our family, so therefore, it is ok to expect the widow to make that provision on our behalf! OR We need money to care for our family, therefore, we give our time and resources to the widow, defend the widow or orphan, and watch God bless us as He promises, for this is His heart. Hearts and motives are never separated from our actions. We can psychologize everything, we can make things really complicated, or we can follow what the Lord teaches us in His word regarding the heart and following actions. Our way of thinking is upside down to God's thinking. In order for our thinking to be right side up, we must constantly align our thinking to Biblical thinking. It is truly a sub-mission of our will to God's will with our whole heart, which in turn affects our motives, resulting in actions, which are pleasing to the Lord. We need to take respon-sibility for our actions and what we say. It is truth and love, which bring healing and encourage the one in distress, to walk through the difficult times with their focus on the Lord, as their sustainer and grace giver.

We all have impact on those that are in the sphere of our life. It is easy to look back with hindsight at what we should have done or should have said. We are given the Bible to teach us how to walk with foresight instead of hindsight. The Bible warns us, guides us, and teaches us how to care for others. The Bible tells us how the Lord will respond to us in the light of our own actions. God's strength and power are given to us in fullness to enable our walk according to the teachings of the Bible.

"May you experience the love of Christ, though it is so great you will never fully understand it. Then you will be filled with the fullness of life and power that comes from God" (Ephesians 3:19, NLT).

Will we walk forward focusing on the advantage we have in Christ and His Word or will we walk forward focusing on the disadvantage that our suffering brings?

I believe that the body of Christ, today, has "Shock Comfort" and "Follow Up Comfort" prepared for any unforeseen event or tragedy. People are great in a crisis. They come from everywhere in their care for the newly bereaved or the one who is ill. A lot of people are right there to help at first, but what kind of help do they offer later? It's the chronic stuff that is still there two years later and three years later that brings me to "Comfort Still Needed". The needs that were originally met and the prayers offered were huge. Prayer is still greatly needed. Quite often, there is still a very large need for bills to be paid that were only temporarily waylaid at the first sign of loss. The widow is still struggling with fear in how she is going to make it. The orphan or widow is still struggling with helplessness and a loss of purpose, even if they are working. The widow is still doing everything herself. Sometimes, it would be helpful and kind to have that stress relieved by another coming alongside. If an orphan or widow, newly bereaved, even several years into be-reavement, were to talk to you, this is what they would say:

Words From an Orphan or Widow
> Please don't be uncomfortable around me.
> Weariness and pain live with me.
> Weep with me.
> Touch me and hug me.
> Emotions and depression sometimes overpower me.

- Listen to me without trying to fix me.
- Don't make fun of me.
- My brain doesn't work very well.
- Listen to me and don't scold me for repeating myself.
- Don't treat me like I am stupid.
- Treat me with dignity.
- Don't encourage me to take drugs to deaden my pain.
- I'm frozen, I don't know what to do.
- Encourage me to trust the Lord.
- Safeguard me in my weakness and vulnerability.
- Don't give me your fears.
- Don't tell me you know what is best for me.
- Please don't change the boundaries God has given me.
- Don't try to figure out why this happened to me.
- Encourage me with grace and truth.
- Help me to hear true warnings.
- When you help me make decisions, don't do it for me.
- Please, don't act like a know-it-all.
- Sometimes I need to be alone.
- My world will never be the same.
- It's too much for me to handle now.

- Encourage me to walk through suffering and walk with me.
- Don't try to make everything better.
- Gently help me to face reality.
- Share your faith and God's faithfulness with me.
- Talk to me about the future.
- Make promises to me and keep them.
- Remember my special days.
- Remember me on holidays.
- Please don't choose friends for me.
- Laugh with me.
- Encourage me to listen to uplifting music.
- When you bring me a meal, stay and eat with me.
- Don't tell me what to do from the outside.
- Please, come into my world and help me.
- Please, help me pay my bills.
- Sometimes I need you to spend time with me.
- Please, don't take advantage of me.
- Please, don't go back to your life after my loved one(s) are buried.
- Don't walk away and leave me.

These words remind us that this person is truly suffering. They need grace and truth. Grace by itself is pure sentiment. Truth by itself is harsh. Grace and truth together bear the tools needed to walk beside the person who is suffering.

The widow whose husband dies after years of illness was a devoted wife. She is now in despair with no money, debt, and no retirement. She is alone and lonely. She feels like she has "no life". She is weak and vulnerable. Proverbs 18:14 says, "The spirit of man can endure his sickness, but a broken spirit who can bear?" How can you comfort her? How can you unburden her? How can you guard her from those that will burden her more and humiliate her more in her humiliation? How can you help her find a new normal? How can you place hope in front of this widow? How can you show her compassion? Have you asked the Lord to increase your compassion?

What Does "Comfort Still Needed" Look Like
- ➤ "Comfort Still Needed" flows out of time spent with the one suffering.
- ➤ Pray and ask for wisdom in comfort, constantly.
- ➤ Assumptions and lack of time kill true compassion.
- ➤ Listen with patience and true compassion.
- ➤ Don't push your opinions onto the one suffering. It is not about you.

- Time spent listening and looking below the surface makes the real need visible.
- Set aside your expectations.
- Don't push, for the weak one may fold after much pushing.
- Always comfort with gentleness, kindness, and patience.
- Ask purposeful questions, such as:
  What did you do today?"
  "How can I help you?"
  "What kinds of things are difficult for you?"
  "Where would you like to go today?"
- Follow up with needed finances.
- Follow up with decision making.
- Drop in for visits.
- Notice house repairs that are needed.
- Eat frequently with the one who is suffering.
- Call on the phone.
- Remember birthdays and holidays.
- Include the one suffering in your family events— enlarge your heart.
- Notice and warn against companions, including family members, with self-interest.
- Encourage the one suffering not to make unnecessary decisions.

- Walk with the one suffering in their pain.
- Encourage putting verses around the house to help one's focus.
- Be careful not to impose your idea of friends.
- Encourage the one suffering to walk within the boundaries God has set.
- Free advice concerning the affairs of the one suffering is not helpful or appreciated.
- Financial and physical care already set up for the one suffering is not your business.
- Encourage listening to music that uplifts.
- Don't belittle the spouse or parent who has passed away.
- Don't portray disbelief that God changed the spouse or parent who died.
- Make sure your warnings are truly for the benefit of the one suffering.
- Respect and dignity breeds true care that is not controlling.
- Refresh the one suffering in their weariness—surprise them.
- Encourage trust and belief in God's faithfulness.
- Allow inabilities that come with both physical and emotional pain.
- Encourage reading and dwelling on scripture.

- ➤ Encourage keeping a journal of thankfulness.
- ➤ Encourage keeping a journal of the Lord's care.
- ➤ Encourage writing the pros and cons of decisions needing to be made.
- ➤ Encourage time spent in prayer.
- ➤ Encourage the living to live.
- ➤ Help the one suffering to find their new normal.
- ➤ Encourage the one living to live without feeling like they need to finish areas that died with their loved one.
- ➤ Encourage the one suffering with life's purpose—to glorify God.
- ➤ Time, time, time—don't walk away after "Follow Up Comfort."

Words To the Orphan and Widow

What if God in His sovereignty gives us a sorrow that never goes away, an illness that will never be healed, or loneliness instead of human companionship? What will you do with what God has given you? Will you honor and worship God with your response or will you bring sorrow to the Lord with your response?

"Delight yourself in the Lord; and He will give you the desires of your heart. Commit your way to the

123

Lord, trust also in Him, and He will do it. And He will bring forth your righteousness as the light, and your judgment as the noonday" (Psalm 37:4-6).

You will continually be faced with choices that are generally founded in the fear of God or the fear of man. There are many causes of fear, such as: fear of the future, fear of abandonment, fear of being alone, fear of not being able to pay your bills, fear of more pain, fear of abuse, and even irrational fear. Truth sets you free. Cling tenaciously to the truths of God. Stop "focusing" on emotions and "focus" on Christ, His faithfulness, His promises, His truth. This means you must stay in the Word of God. Cry out to the Lord for wisdom.

"Now she who is a widow indeed, and who has been left alone has fixed her hope on God. Night and day she asks God for help and spends much time in prayer" (I Timothy 5:5).

Be on your guard. Remember that God is an observer and a helper to the one suffering. What someone does to the one suffering He sees and He takes particular care of the one suffering.

"Do not rob the poor because he is poor, or crush the afflicted at the gate; for the Lord will plead their case, and take the life of those who rob them" (Proverbs 22:22, 23).

Ultimately, everything comes down to where you place your affections. Are your affections set on how something looks, on things, on others, on time fillers, on television, on your plan, on the purpose you had for your life, or are your affections set on Christ? Your care is not based on your circumstances. Your care is based on the "Lord of the Armies of Heaven" who created and set the boundaries for the heavens, for the sea, for your suffering, for your orphanage, and for your widowhood.

Advice For the Orphan and Widow
- ➤ Rely on God's strength.
- ➤ Stay in church and a Christian community.
- ➤ Remember that the Lord is there to listen and give strength.
- ➤ Repent of sins God brings to your mind.
- ➤ Take the time to grieve.
- ➤ Don't use drugs or alcohol to deaden the pain.
- ➤ Keep putting one foot in front of the other.

- Don't make any major decisions until your mind is clear.
- Don't make unnecessary decisions.
- Don't let your remaining family or relatives control your life.
- Walk only with good companions that will safeguard you.
- Guard yourself from so called friends and family who are self serving.
- Make a list of all the things your spouse or parents did. Take this list and write down how each area can be resolved.
- Complete unfinished areas in your home, if you are able.
- Stay busy and work.
- Don't allow others to sidetrack you from your responsibilities.
- Plan something different to do on difficult memory days and holidays.
- Write down what matters to you.
- Write down what is difficult for you to handle.
- Cry out to the Lord for wisdom and direction.
- Seek counsel, if needed, without listening to the "many" voices.

- Don't be quick to believe the "many" voices without checking credibility.
- Do you ask the Lord what He has for you today?
- Do you mourn the loss of yesterday?
- On what do you set your affections?
- Watch out for the little things that will erode your faith.
- Psalms is a wonderful book to read.
- Keep a journal and daily write down what you are thankful for. This will ease doubts and fears.
- Keep a journal and daily write down how the Lord is taking care of you.
- When you wake up from your suffering, will you be happy with the decisions you made, even if you married again?

Why are you living? Are you more concerned about focusing on your journey or relying on the strength and help of the Lord?

******

The Bible states the need to care for the widow or orphan 47-48 times. It also states very clearly God's view of "anyone" that takes advantage of or refuses care for a widow or orphan. Let this verse be a reminder of how seriously God regards the love and care given to the widow or orphan.

"You shall not afflict any widow or orphan. If you afflict him at all, and if he does cry out to Me, I will surely hear his cry; and My anger will be kindled, and I will kill you with the sword, and your wives shall become widows and your children fatherless" (Exodus 22:22-24).

CHAPTER 10

Just In Case You Asked

"Though you have made me
see troubles, many and bitter,
you will restore my life again;
from the depths of the earth
you will again bring me up."
—Psalm 71:20, NIV

In each life, God designs the scars and blessings to bring glory to Himself. God also designs suffering to grow the Christian up into maturity in Him, to prepare the Christian for service, and to prepare the Christian to bear up under the weight of God's glory when called home to heaven. Knowing the reasons for suffering somehow gives purpose to all of the difficult areas that I walk through and am "in" currently. Knowing the reasons for suffering also gives me courage to bear up under all types of suffering. As I look back at so many hard things written in these pages and many more that are not written down, I am reminded of these verses in Romans 8:28-39:

"And we know that God causes all things to work together for good to those who love God, to those who are called according to His purpose. For whom He foreknew, He also predestined to become conformed to the image of His Son, that He might be the firstborn among many brethren; and whom He predestined, these He also called; and whom He called, these He also justified; and whom He justified, these He also glorified. What then shall we say to these things? If God is for us, who is against us? He who did not spare His own Son, but delivered Him up for us all, how will He not also with Him freely give us all things? Who will bring a charge against God's elect? God is the one who justifies; who is the one who condemns? Christ Jesus is He who died, yes, rather, who was raised, who is at the right hand of God, who also intercedes for us. Who shall separate us from the love of Christ? Shall tribulation, or distress, or persecution, or famine, or nakedness, or peril, or sword? Just as it is written, 'For Thy sake we are being put to death all day long; we were considered as sheep to be slaughtered.' But all these things we overwhelmingly conquer through Him who loved us. For I am convinced that neither death, nor life, nor angels, nor principalities, nor things present, nor things to come, nor powers, nor height, nor depth, nor any other created thing, shall be able to separate us from the <u>love</u> of God, which is in Christ Jesus our Lord."

Wow! I am overwhelmed with the particular love of Christ that He has given me and His declaration of faithfulness.

One of the huge blessings that God gave me early in my Christian life was the knowledge and understanding of His sovereign providence, which governs all of life. God is not capricious, nor is He vindictive. An understanding of God's providence has enabled me to say with Job, "The Lord has given and the Lord has taken away. Blessed be the name of the Lord" (Job 1:21). In fact, soon after Matt and Anna's deaths, my son made a shield with Job's response (my response) printed on it. We put this shield on all of our vehicles.

Anger has not been part of my suffering. I do desire to please the Lord with all of my heart and that desire only continues to increase. I have walked with mourning over the many areas in which He has forgiven me. I have struggled in many areas emotionally. Pain is agony. Losing part of your family is agony. Losing the hope of future with your family, on this earth, has been agony. Depression, forgetfulness, exhaustion, weeping, loneliness, isolation, poor judgment, wanting to give up, and learning to live with a "new normal" have all been part of my struggle.

Thanksgiving given to the Lord is so freeing. As I look back in thankfulness, I am most thankful for having my feet unplanted from this earth. It is through suffering that we truly begin to know how much the Lord loves us. It is also through suffering that we see glimpses of God's holiness and how far we fall short in our walk of holiness. This also brings us to praise for the cleansing effect brought about by suffering.

When I think of my husband, who is no longer my husband, I see that he is now truly free in Christ, perfected in holiness, and bearing up under the weight of God's glory. As I think about my daughter, I know that she is safe. Anna doesn't live with me anymore. She lives in heaven with the Lord. She is truly glorified. I praise the Lord that He has taken two of His children home to be with

Him. That praise is also effective for any reader who has a loved one now home with the Lord.

Each fall, until Christmas, there is a minor crescendo that builds within my heart. There is a residual sadness that crops up at unexpected times and sometimes over-whelms my spirit. Christmas was always a special time for me. Now, Christmas is one of the most difficult times of the year. I just want Christmas to come and go as quickly as possible so that life can continue without thoughts of that horrific time.

The Lord gave me a very special gift the Christmas of 2004. My son had been teasing me about a Christmas present he had for me. Not being able to wait until Christmas, he called me to come and see his gift. I was astounded. He built for me the most beautiful red oak dresser, with a three tier mirror. It was the first piece of furniture he had ever built and his craftsmanship was superb. In the twenty-two years I was married, I never had a dresser in which to put my clothes. This was such a huge blessing.

It has been ten years now since my family's home going. It took over eight years to be able to think clearly. I may have appeared normal to others, but was definitely not inside. Thinking and making decisions was disaster. Learning anything new was a joke. Retaining information was not a possibility. The weeping continued for at least five years. Even now a thought, a circumstance, an event, or another person freshly bereaved will cause weeping. There have been many difficulties along the way these past ten years. Not everyone is kind. There are those who abuse and take advantage of the weak and suffering, seeing gain for themselves. As suffering stretches on over time there may be one or two faithful friends, faithful and godly friends, who truly cover suffering with compassion and love. There are no expectations from these kinds of friends. There is delight and care in their friendship. Godly love is light and not burdensome. This kind of love brings encouragement and gentle reminders of trust in the Lord Jesus who suffered far more than I have suffered.

Time passes so quickly. Looking back, I see that I have just been putting one foot in front of the other and the Lord has been directing my steps. The Lord has touched me with a sent card, a phone call, or an email when the loneliness was great. The Lord has given tasks to help others so that the loss was not in the forefront. He put other people in front of me that needed comfort, even though I still needed comfort. He has continually reminded me of the brevity of life. He has restored belongings in miraculous ways, which have been abused by others. He has blessed so richly by taking things that were undone for years, causing them to get finished, and causing the use of them to bring refreshment to others. There is peace!

I am living. I have goals and plans that are all subject to the Lord's will. I am not the same person that I was ten years ago. I still struggle with my rib, my hip and my immune system. Regular visits to a chiropractor keep my pain to a minimum. I walk with a residual sadness. I feel the pain of others. I am sober, though I do have joy. I have seen the Lord keep His promises. I am even more certain that the Lord can be trusted.

It is in suffering and brokenness that I have seen the face of my Savior. It is in suffering that I have seen the magnitude of His love and care. There are times that I have just crawled up into the lap of my Savior, where there is safety and rest. He takes care of me. Sometimes, He carries me when I can't walk. Other times, He holds my hand and helps me walk. I would not trade one bit of the suffering He has brought into my life, for the reality of being with the Lord. It is through suffering that I have seen glimpses of His glory. And then, there is the "hope" that one day I will see my Savior face to face and this suffering will be finished. Truly, there will be the pure joy of being in His presence. For now, I see Him in the Bible. I see Him in my afflictions. I see Him in my fellow brothers and sisters in Christ. I wait with patience for the day I will be with Him. There is a great cloud of witnesses, of all those who have gone before us that have attained that realized hope. This gives me great encouragement to press on. Time is continuing to pass and the Lord is preparing me for that weight of His glory.

CHAPTER 11

Helpful Questions

"How precious is thy lovingkindness, O God!
and the children of men
take refuge in the shadow of thy wings."
—Psalm 36:7

The One Suffering

➢ Who or what does my heart love above all else?

➢ What are my desires for life?

➢ What do I want my suffering to accomplish?

➢ Am I more concerned about the circumstances of my suffering or am I concerned about walking in integrity, even if it is to my own hurt?

➢ Will I escape the pain of suffering at all cost?

➢ Will I stay in a hard place, rather than fleeing?

➢ Will I trust God to bring my redemption?

➢ How am I responding to others in my life while suffering?

➢ How am I responding to the expectations that others have for me?

- Am I putting into practice the "fruit of the Spirit" during these difficult times?
- Am I complaining or thanking?
- Am I full of self-pity?
- Am I angry?
- Do I realize that anger questions the Goodness of God?
- Have I repented of my anger?
- What do I need to repent of now?
- Did God take something I want?
- Did God not give me something or someone I want?
- Do I know better than God what I need?
- What are my expectations?
- Are my expectations reasonable?
- What kind of companions do I keep?
- Do my companions encourage me to walk in Godliness?
- Do my companions encourage me in worldly philosophy?
- Do my companions take advantage of me?
- Do my companions abuse me in my suffering?
- Do I have companions who will give trustworthy advice?

- Do I have companions that safeguard me in my weakness?
- How am I responding to God?
- Do I question the Goodness of God?
- Am I distrusting of God's Providence in my life?
- Am I trusting God no matter what the outcome?
- Am I trusting God with my expectations for the outcome?
- Do I believe that God is merciful?
- Is my highest desire to bring glory to the Lord in my suffering?
- Do I meditate, memorize, and dwell on the Word of God?
- Will I pray for daily grace and strength?
- What is the next faithful step?
- Lord, what do you want me to do now?

The One Comforting

> ➢ What expectations does the one suffering have from me?
>
> ➢ What expectations do I have for the one who is suffering?
>
> ➢ Should I have expectations for the one who is suffering?
>
> ➢ Am I expecting the one suffering to do something for me?
>
> ➢ How am I viewing the belongings of the one suffering?
>
> ➢ Do I have compassion for the one suffering?
>
> ➢ Do I look to place hope in front of the one suffering and to follow through with that hope?
>
> ➢ Do I grumble and complain about meeting another's needs?
>
> ➢ Do I grumble and complain about the weaknesses in the one suffering?
>
> ➢ Do I seek to cover the weakness in the one suffering with love?

- Do I refuse to place another's needs before my own?
- What kind of companions do I have?
- What kind of companion am I to the one who is suffering?
- What does the length of my comforting look like?
- Will my comfort be founded in Scripture or worldly philosophy?
- Am I comforting for recognition?
- Am I comforting out of the Lord's comfort He has given me?
- Am I comforting with understanding, knowledge, and love?
- Is my love for Christ displayed in how I love the one suffering?
- Am I coming alongside the one suffering where they live?
- Am I expecting the one suffering to come into my life so I can comfort them?
- What is my view of God in any affliction?
- Will I encourage full trust in a Sovereign God?
- Will I guard my words with kindness and gentleness?
- Will I give trustworthy advice?

- Will my advice be given for my advantage?
- Is my advice appropriate for the one suffering?
- Is my advice appropriate for me and not for the one suffering?
- Will I judge the one suffering or leave the judgment to God?
- Will I listen and listen and listen to the one suffering?
- Do I encourage thankfulness for the Providence of God?
- Will I pray with and for the one suffering?
- Will I encourage the meditation and memorization of the Word of God?
- Will I treat the one suffering with dignity?

******

"O Lord, who may abide in Thy tent? Who may dwell on Thy holy hill? He who walks with integrity, and works righteousness, and speaks truth in his heart. He does not slander with his tongue, nor does evil to his neighbor, nor takes up a reproach against his friend; in whose eyes a reprobate is despised, but who honors those who fear the Lord; he swears to his own hurt, and does not change; he does not put out his money at interest, nor does he take a bribe against the innocent. He who does these things will never be shaken" (Psalm 15).

"But the fruit of the Spirit is love, joy, peace, patience, kindness, goodness, faithfulness, gentleness, and self-control" (Galatians 5:22-23).

"If I speak in the tongues of men or of angels, but do not have love, I am only a resounding gong or a clanging cymbal. If I have the gift of prophecy and can fathom all mysteries and all knowledge, and if I have a faith that can move mountains, but have not love, I am nothing. If I give all I possess to the poor and give over my body to hardship that I may boast, but do not have love, I gain nothing. Love is patient, love is kind. It does not envy, it does not boast, it is not proud. It does not dishonor others, it is not self-seeking, it is not easily angered, it keeps no record of wrongs. Love does not delight in evil but rejoices with the truth. It always protects, always trusts, always hopes, always perseveres. Love never fails. But where there are prophecies, they will cease; where there are tongues, they will be stilled; where there is knowledge, it will pass away. For we know in part and we prophesy in part, but when completeness comes, what is in part disappears. When I was a child, I talked like a child, I thought like a child, I reasoned like a child. When I became a man, I put the ways of childhood behind me. For now we see only a reflection as in a mirror; then we shall see face to face. Now I know in part; then I shall know fully, even as I am fully known. And now these three remain: faith, hope, and love. But the greatest of these is love."

(I Corinthians 13; NIV)

CHAPTER 12

Do You Know?

As you read through the chapters of this book, you may have realized that there is a "key" which unlocks the way one walks through suffering of any type. That key is "hope". You may also remember the many references to God, Jesus, the God/man, the Lord, and Christ as the basis of that "hope." It is with these names that we begin our story.

Our story begins, with the first man and the first woman, at the creation of the world. In the first two chapters of Genesis, the first book in the Bible, we are told how God created the heavens and the earth, the darkness and the light (that was the first day); the heavens and the waters (that was the second day); the dry land, sea, and vegetation (that was the third day); the seasons, the sun, and the moon (that was the fourth day); the water creatures and the birds (that was the fifth day); the animals, the creeping things, the first man and woman (that was the sixth day); and a day of rest (that was the seventh day). God created man and woman in perfection. They had no knowledge of wrong doing. The first man, Adam, and the first woman, Eve, lived in the beautiful Garden of Eden. God told them they could eat everything in the garden "except" the fruit from one tree—the tree of knowledge of good and evil. There was a crafty serpent (Satan) that twisted the words of God and tempted Eve into eating the forbidden fruit. Eve chose to eat of the forbidden fruit. Adam also ate some of the fruit, which was given to him by Eve. As soon as they ate the fruit, they had understanding of right and wrong. When God came to walk with them in the cool of the day, Adam and Eve were hiding in shame, for they knew they had sinned. As a result of Adam's sin, God threw them out of the beautiful Garden of Eden.

As the first man, Adam is the head of the entire human race. God described the consequences of Adam's sin, which are passed down to all mankind. God declared that there would be difficulties and sufferings throughout life, which would finally end in death. The magnitude of Adam's sin comes down to the fact, that now, each one of us, is born "in sin"—Adam's sin is our sin. Each of us is a sinner. It is just as if we were there with Adam and committed his sin. This does not leave us with hope! This does leave us with all of the illness, pain, suffering, and death that we see all around us!

"This is the history of the descendants of Adam. When God created people, He made them in the likeness of God" (Genesis 5:1, NLT).

"When Adam sinned, sin entered the entire human race. Adam's sin brought death, so death spread to everyone, for everyone sinned" (Romans 5:12, NLT).

"For all have sinned and fall short of the glory of God" (Romans 3:23).

"Therefore, just as through one man sin entered into the world, and death through sin, and so death spread to all men, because all sinned—" (Romans 5:12).

But, there is "hope". Before the world was ever created there was God the Father, God the Son (Jesus Christ), and God the Holy Spirit (the Comforter). They are one God in three persons and three different roles. There was a plan within the three persons of God. This plan was to redeem from sin a multitude (a great number) of people, from every tribe and language of the human race. This redemption was enacted and accomplished by sending

God the Son (Jesus) to be born as a man (the God/man) so that He could live a perfect life of righteousness. Jesus was 100% still God and simultaneously 100% man. To complete His life as a man, Jesus was crucified. God's wrath was poured out on Jesus as He was crucified for being a sinner, though He had not sinned. He took all of "our" sins on Himself and then He died. Because He was still God, He rose again from the dead, conquering death. After this, Jesus went back up to Heaven and sat down at the right hand of God the Father. In this seat, Jesus continually prays for those that He has redeemed. Those of us who are redeemed, have repented of our sins, and now desire to love the Lord God with all of our being. Our redemption is another picture of the "hope" that we have.

"For while we were still helpless, at the right time Christ died for the ungodly. For one will hardly die for a righteous man; though perhaps for the good man someone would dare even to die. But God demonstrates His own love toward us, in that while we were yet sinners, Christ died for us. Much more then, having now been justified by His blood, we shall be saved from the wrath of God through Him. For if while we were enemies, we were reconciled to God through the death of His Son, much more, having been reconciled, we shall be saved by His life. And not only this, but we also exult in God through our Lord Jesus Christ, through whom we have now received the reconciliation" (Romans 5:6-11).

Jesus' life of righteousness (perfect living), His death, and His resurrection from the dead, is payment for our sin. This places squarely in front of us the only "hope" that is truly available to all of us, who will repent of our sins, accept the forgiveness of Jesus—this sinless God/man who died for you and me—and worship Him as the only true God. When we repent of our sins, Jesus gives us His righteousness. God the Father no longer looks at us and sees our sin. Instead, when God the Father looks at us, He sees the righteousness of His Son, Jesus, covering our sins. God no longer remembers our sins.

"For as through the one man's disobedience the many were made sinners, even so through the obedience of the One the many will be made righteous" (Romans 5:19).

As I have been reading lately, I keep running across this phrase: "The Lord of the Armies of Heaven". We saw the power of God in creation. He spoke and everything was created (Genesis 1). Much of the Bible teaches us of the character and glory of God. Remember, there is ONE God in three persons--God the Father, God the Son (Jesus our Redeemer), and God the Holy Spirit (our Comforter). God is awesome and holy. God hates sin. God will pour out His wrath on sinners. One day, all of us who have not repented of our sins will die and go to Hell—a place prepared by God for those that hate Him. Those of us that have repented of our sins and love God will be in Heaven with Jesus when we die.

Now (if we know Jesus), when we suffer with pain, affliction, and the death of loved ones, we have "hope". The Holy Spirit is our comforter. Jesus is praying for us and bringing our prayers to God the Father. The great love and care we have from the three Gods in One is so amazing.

If we do not repent, we do <u>NOT</u> have any real "hope". We have <u>no</u> "hope" of comfort and help in suffering in this life; nor do we have any "hope" in death. We are assured of more suffering in the fiery pits of Hell as God pours out His wrath on us for sinning against Him.

If you are burdened with your guilt, here is the hand of Jesus reaching out to save you. Jesus is the Savior who calls you to Himself. He will free you from your sins. He will meet you in your need. His love is powerful. You cannot forgive your sins. Jesus is the only one that has the power to forgive your sins and restore life to you. You cannot earn or work your way to Jesus. You are a prisoner of your sin—a debtor. You cannot free yourself. Call out to Jesus. Ask Him to forgive your sins. Ask Him to free you!

"For Whoever will call upon the name of the Lord will be saved" (Romans 10:13).

"Dear Jesus, I have sinned (name your sins) against you. Please forgive my sins and cover me with your righteousness. Please don't remember my sins any more. Please change my heart to love you and worship you with every part of my being. In Jesus Name, Amen."

"For when you were slaves of sin, you were free in regard to righteousness. Therefore what benefit were you then deriving from the things of which you are now ashamed? For the outcome of those things is death. But now having been freed from sin and enslaved to God, you derive your benefit, resulting in sanctification, and the outcome, eternal life. For the wages of sin is death, but the free gift of God is eternal life in Christ Jesus our Lord" (Romans 6:20-23).

"For by grace you have been saved through faith; and that not of yourselves, it is the gift of God; not as a result of works, that no one should boast" (Ephesians 2:8-9).

"If we confess our sins, He is faithful and righteous to forgive us our sins and to cleanse us from all unrighteousness" (I John 1:9).

If you have just repented of your sins, please feel free to let us or another Christian know. May God Bless you.

Feel free to contact us

www.amsosad.com

support@amsosad.com

"I Am With You"

I am with you, says the Father;
Through the floods, I calm and keep.
Though the swelling waves surround you,
I surround the waters deep.
Fear not, loved one; feel My presence.
You will never be alone.
Trust me, loved one; you are precious.
You are Mine—My very own.

I am with you, says the Savior,
Even to the age's end.
Never leaving, nor forsaking,
I'm your ever-present Friend.
Fear not, loved one; hear My comfort:
None can pluck you from My hand.
Trust me, loved one; I am constant:
None can change what I have planned.

I am with you, says the Spirit,

There is nowhere you can flee.

Neither height nor depth can hide you;

Every place is home to Me.

Fear not, loved one; hear My witness:

You are God's own child and heir.

Trust me, loved one; hear My whisper:

Deep within you, I am here.

Come be with Me, says the Master,

Greeting hopeful, homesick eyes.

I was with you in your journey;

Be with Me in paradise.

Fear not, loved one; know My promise:

I will surely, quickly come.

Trust me, loved one; know My purpose:

I will bring you safely home.

Dedicated to Colonial Hills Baptist Church of Indianapolis, IN in
remembrance of July 27, 2013.

www.ingramcontent.com/pod-product-compliance
Lightning Source LLC
Chambersburg PA
CBHW071445090426
42737CB00011B/1782